THE SACRAMENTAL MAGIC OF EASTER

THE SACRAMENTAL MAGIC OF EASTER
A Guide to Christian Ceremonial
Ritual During Lent and Easter

by
Stephen Mandes Thomas

AEON

First published in 2026 by
Aeon Books

Copyright © 2026 by Stephen Mandes Thomas

The right of Stephen Mandes Thomas to be identified as the author of this work has been asserted in accordance with §§ 77 and 78 of the Copyright Design and Patents Act 1988.

All rights reserved. No part of this publication may be reproduced, stored in a retrieval system, or transmitted, in any form or by any means, electronic, mechanical, photocopying, recording, or otherwise, without the prior written permission of the publisher.

British Library Cataloguing in Publication Data

A C.I.P. for this book is available from the British Library

ISBN-13: 978-1-80152-222-9

Typeset by Medlar Publishing Solutions Pvt Ltd, India

www.aeonbooks.co.uk

CONTENTS

CHAPTER ONE

Introduction	1
How to use this book	4
Terminology and definitions	5
Getting started	13

CHAPTER TWO

The foundations of Christian magic	17
Foundational practice 1: A prayer rule	18
Foundational practice 2: Banishing	19
Foundational practice 3: *Lectio divina*	22
Foundational practice 4: Opening a magical temple	24

CHAPTER THREE

An overview of the seasons of Lent and Easter	29
The history of Lent	29
The structure of Lent and Easter	31
Gesimatide	33
Shrove Tuesday	41

CHAPTER FOUR

Lent	45
The Nature and purpose of Lent	46
Lenten practice	49
Ash Wednesday	62
The First Sunday of Lent	67
The Second Sunday of Lent	74
The Third Sunday of Lent	80
The Fourth Sunday of Lent	88
Passion Sunday and Passiontide	97

CHAPTER FIVE

The Easter Triduum	109
Holy Week practice	109
Maundy Thursday	110
Good Friday	115
Holy Saturday: The Harrowing of Hell	118

CHAPTER SIX

Easter and Eastertide	127
Easter	127
Paschaltide and the Sundays after Easter	133
Ascension Thursday	135
Pentecost	139

AFTERWORD

	143

APPENDIXES

	145
Appendix 1: Sources and further reading	145
Appendix 2: A selection of common prayers	148
Appendix 3: An Easter Calendar	160

BIBLIOGRAPHY

	163

INDEX

	165

CHAPTER ONE

Introduction

The death and Resurrection of Jesus Christ is the central moment in the Christian religion. The holiday which commemorates the Resurrection is, therefore, the central moment in the Christian year.

The previous book in this series focused on the seasons of Christmas and Advent. In that book, I pointed out that in our modern world Advent has been reduced from a fast (punctuated by occasional feasts) to a shopping season, and Christmas has been reduced from a 12-day celebration to a single day, and very often a single morning.

Easter's fate has been a bit different. The Roman Catholic Church and some of the other Sacramental churches still keep the penitential season of Lent, though its severity has been much reduced. As there isn't as much shopping to be done, the secular world largely ignores Lent, except for the return of fish sandwiches at McDonald's. Easter itself, since it already falls on the weekend, barely merits a day off from work or school. Churches still make a big deal about it, as they necessarily must, and many families at least preserve the traditional Easter Dinner. As in the case of Advent and Christmastime, however, the paschal season (to give it its traditional name) and its many feasts and fasts has been greatly reduced in our popular culture. Easter Monday is frequently ignored, and the days of Ascension and Pentecost are remembered only by the increasingly small fraction of our population that still goes to church on Sunday.

All of this is one manifestation of a larger problem, which can be called the *disenchantment of the world*. This is a concept which originated in the work of early sociologists, particularly Max Weber.

This book, and the series of which it is a part, is intended as a work of *re-enchantment*.

This is hardly the first book to take this approach. Indeed, in many circles "re-enchantment" is now something of a cliche. Moreover, it's not actually clear that the "disenchantment" that Weber discussed ever really happened. In spite of all the "scientific" and "rational" pretensions of the modern world, most people still live in a world in which magic is real, psychic phenomena occur, and spirits exist. Fear of ridicule keeps most people from speaking about it in public, but if you talk to people one-on-one, or in a small group in which they feel safe, just about everyone turns out to have a story about an encounter with a ghost or a nature spirit, a prophetic dream, a grandmother who could heal the sick with her prayers. In terms of our view of the world, we don't really need "re-enchantment." What we really need is just to be left alone by the small population of academics, journalists, and their sycophants who are the only people that truly live in the "disenchanted world."

There is one part of life, however, which has been thoroughly disenchanted, to the point that many people aren't even aware of it. And that is the matter of *time*.

Our ancestors, pagan as well as Christian, lived in a world defined by *rhythm*. Nature itself provided the framework, dimming the lights and the thermostat in the Winter and turning both up high in the summer. But the temporal rhythm was not defined only by nature. The Christian tradition, like the pagan tradition that it subsumed and baptized, has historically been defined by the liturgical calendar. Saints' days and other feast days were kept and celebrated with pageantry and processions, bonfires and magical rituals. Christmas and Easter, Pentecost and Michaelmas were seasons of great celebration. Advent, Lent, and the minor fasts of Saint Michael's Lent and Saint Martin's Lent were penitential seasons, characterized by fasting from meat and the Confession of sins. In this respect, the Christian world was continuous with the pagan world, which also had its sacred times and seasons, its times of penitence and fasting, lucky days and days of ill fortune. It is only the modern world that has attempted to flatten all time into one continuous working day, broken up only by weekends (for the lucky) and paid vacation days, taken at random throughout the year.

This purpose of this work, then, and the series of which it is a part, is precisely the *re-enchantment of time*. As the previous book in this series focused on Advent and Christmas, this book focuses on Lent and Easter. There are three goals or aims which underlie the work ahead:

First, we're going to explore the traditions of Lent and Easter. We'll pay special attention to older customs that have been lost or minimized in modern times. Doctrinal Catholics and other Christians who prefer an orthodox approach to their religion will probably find this the most useful part.

The previous book in this series, *The Sacramental Magic of Advent*, included details on the many saints' days celebrated during Advent and Christmastime. I've decided to forgo that for the sake of this book. This season is much longer than the previous one, and it the dates vary much more broadly. The earliest possible date for Septuagesima, which begins the pre-Lent season, is January 10, while the latest possible date for Pentecost is June 5! The many saints' days and other feasts of the Church, such as the Annunciation, which are not explicitly part of Lent or Easter, will, therefore, be covered in a future volume.

Second, we're going to explore an alternative interpretation of Lent, Easter, and the entire nature of the Christian Mystery tradition. Many Christian practitioners of magic and Esotericism find the traditional interpretation of Easter and the Death and Resurrection of Christ unsatisfying. Some ideas, such as the "penal substitution theory," which suggests that God was furious with mankind but took it out on His son, we find, at best, hard to swallow. Other ideas, equally mainstream but sometimes under-emphasized, such as the Franciscan theory of the Atonement, we find more plausible but still not quite completely satisfying. Using the lens of the mythical interpretation of Christian history and the magical model of the Planes of Being, we will explore a deeper theory of the Resurrection and of the nature of Salvation that I believe Esoteric Christians will find more satisfying.

Finally, just as in the previous book, we will present a complete system of initiation into the work of Christian magic and the Christian Mysteries. This is a deeper and more challenging initiation than the one given in the Christmas book. It builds on the work presented in that book in the same way that the cycle of Easter builds on the cycle of Christmas. If you want to follow this path, I strongly recommend that you complete the Christmas initiation first. That said, if that's not possible—if, say, you bought this book in January, and don't want to wait until next year before reading it—you will still find much of value in the chapters on magic, ritual, and initiation, and you can still work with many of the practices presented. Some of it, however, should be left until you've completed the work of Christmas and the Initiation of Epiphany. If that's the case, don't worry. It just means you'll get to work through this book twice at least, and you'll get more out of it the second time around.

How to use this book

This book presents a series of meditations and magical practices designed to attune the soul of the initiate to the energies of the Easter season within the system of Sacramental Magic. These practices build on one another in sequence, culminating with a final initiation at Pentecost.

Some books of magic are designed to be undertaken at any time, but this one is specifically keyed to the seasons of Lent and Easter. We begin at Septuagesima, three Sundays prior to the start of Lent. It will be best if you can start the work on time, but if you're unable to—if you purchased this book after the start of Lent, say—you should feel free to jump in at any time prior to Passiontide, which is the Fifth Sunday of Lent. I don't recommend starting any later than that: Easter will come again next year, and you can keep this book on the shelf until then.

If you have already worked through one or both of the previous books in this series—*The Book of Sacramental Magic* or *The Sacramental Magic of Advent*—then you already have a strong foundation of practice upon which to build. You should still review the introductory material, but most of it will already be familiar to you.

If, instead, you are new to this work, you should read all of the introductory material and the section entitled "Foundations of Christian Magic" before proceeding. Make sure that you're prepared for the work ahead.

On the other hand, if the number of practices and the level of commitment seem daunting, don't despair. You can always do what you are able to this year, and then build on that in the years to come.

The reality is that the number of practices given in this book, especially for the Sundays of Lent and the Easter Triduum, may seem daunting to anyone, even those who are already experienced in this work. This is especially true if you also have the demands of work and family to occupy your time. Again, don't despair. Easter is going to come again next year, and the year after that, and the year after that. The first time you work through this book, you should do as much as you can, with the tools that you have available. When Lent comes back around again next year, you may find that you are able to do more. On the other hand, you may find that, rather than "more," it is a different set of practices which calls out to you. Of course, between now and next year, you may find yourself in a very different situation, perhaps with a more demanding job, perhaps with a larger family. In that case, you can scale your practice back and do less than before. The rule is always: Do what you can with what you have.

Terminology and definitions

This book uses terminology with which a reader unfamiliar with the larger world of alternative spirituality may not be familiar. Moreover, there are certain common terms which are used herein in a sense different to that common in ordinary speech. It will therefore be helpful to define our terms here at the outset, so that there will be no confusion going forward.

On the other hand, to use a single translation runs the risk of entangling us too much in the collective energies—or *egregore*, to use the occult term—of the traditions and groups of which they are a part. The King James Bible is used in the Anglican and many other Protestant churches, while the Douay-Rheims is the favorite of the Traditionalist movement within Roman Catholicism. All of these groups have both their virtues and their problems or besetting sins, and the goal is to use the traditional material without becoming entangled in traditional problems. The use of multiple translations helps to overcome that potential pitfall.

Let's start with *magic*, as this is the most controversial of them all. The Catholic Church defines "magic" as the accomplishment of supernatural effects with the aid of any spirit other than God. Now, it's clear from that definition that the "spirits other than God" don't include the saints or angels, both of which are regularly invoked by the Catholic faithful. This is the case because the saints and angels are not truly "other than God," because their powers are derived from God and are, ultimately, the power of God manifesting through particular spiritual channels. No, what the Church means by this definition is "accomplishing supernatural effects with the aid of demons or other evil spirits." So let's state from the outset that, by this definition, there will be no magic in this book.

Of course, this isn't what we usually mean by the term magic. Some people may want to quibble over this—in the age of the internet, there are people available to argue about anything—but it's a fact of life and history that words change their meaning over time. And so, in everyday use, "magic" simply means "anything wonderful or fantastic or hinting at the supernatural."

And of course, there is a third definition of magic, which is used by practitioners. According to this definition, magic is: "The art and science of causing changes in consciousness in accordance with will." We discussed this definition in the previous volume in this series, but right now I'd like to break it down further. And so let's go through it one term at a time.

Foremost, magic is an art and a science. When we say that it is a science, we mean that it is based on certain principles which can be known to the rational mind. We'll discuss these principles as we go on. When we say that it is an art, we mean two things. First, like any art, it is intended to produce certain effects. A painter paints paintings; a musician makes music; and a magician performs magical workings. Second, like any art, magic has an irreducibly personal element. Painting is done according to certain methods, but it also requires the effort of an individual painter, whose work will be unlike that of any other painter. Finally, every art, ultimately, draws on powers which are above the individual. Truly great visual art, music, and literature is not really created only by the individual painter, musician, or writer. Great art is, in some sense, inspired by powers above the individual. This is why poets from ancient times and down through the Christian era until the modern day begin their works by calling on the Muses. The Muses are spirits who inspire artists; in Christian works, calling on the Muses is often a metaphor for calling on the Holy Spirit. Of course, we may assume that the Holy Spirit acts through angelic Muses, since God always works through the angels.

Second, the aim of magic is to produce *changes* in *consciousness*. This is critical, because it defines the field on which a magician operates. A painter's tools are paints and brushes; their field is a canvas.

A musician's tool is their instrument and musical theory; their field is sound. A magician's tool is their own mind and the larger world of the mind in general, and this is the field on which he operates. Moreover, the end of magic is a *change* in consciousness. We practice magic because we don't want things to remain the way they are.

Please notice that, by this definition, magic is very common. Indeed, magic is around us all the time. The Mass itself is a work of magic. Performed correctly, it is intended to have a great effect on the consciousness—that is to say, the soul—of every person who participates in it. All of the Sacraments are great works of magic. Indeed, the Sacraments are a special kind of High Magic called Mysteries. More on this in a moment.

There are other forms of magic being performed all around us, all the time. Some of these are helpful or at least neutral, but many are harmful. I'm not only talking about the obvious works of summoning demons and casting curses, though these have become unfortunately common in recent years, especially among people who ought to know better. Advertisements on TV and the internet are forms of magic, intended to shape the consciousness of the person who sees the ad according to the will of the advertiser. Moreover, things like movies, TV programs, and popular music are also magical in their own way. Consider the way that musical genres like punk rock can turn an ordinary 15-year-old into someone with a mohawk, a leather jacket, and a bad attitude directed at anyone with any authority. This is magic. Have you ever watched a movie and felt yourself transformed by it? That was magic too, for good or ill. I once had an experience where a number of friends of mine went out and saw a movie, and after that came home convinced that I was their enemy, because I reminded them of the bad guys in the movie. That sounds absurd, but it really happened. That's magic, and it's evil magic. And that's also another reason to practice magic yourself: If you can control your own consciousness, it becomes much harder for other people to control it for you.

Finally, these changes in consciousness are made in accordance with will. Here we have to be very clear. Some critics of magic have claimed that the emphasis on will is a form of the will to power, and that magic has to do with increasing one's power over others and bludgeoning the universe into giving us what we want. This is, in fact, how evil magic works, but when it comes to the High Magic we are discussing here, nothing could be further from the truth.

Magical theory often speaks of the True Will of the magician and the importance of finding one's True Will. As Esoteric Christians, we totally accept this theory, but we add an important qualification. The True Will of the magician or of any person is precisely the Will of God for that person. It is not our True Will to indulge in drink or drugs, to philander or cheat on our spouses, to waste our money on gambling or on frivolities, to avoid completing the great projects we set out for ourselves by wasting time on the internet or on video games. We experience impulses to do these things. These impulses are called the passions, and the work of discovering our True Will is identical with the work of becoming the master of our passions. Our passions arise, ultimately, from our animal nature. To obey them is to be a slave to them, and to other people (such as advertisers) who are good at manipulating them.

I once heard an Eastern Orthodox Christian, a recent convert to that religion, claim that in Christianity magic is forbidden because magic "entangles us in the passions." This is simply not true, for the reasons already stated. Indulging the passions, whether they aim at sex or drink or money, is precisely the opposite of the Will of God.

And so that's magic.

What about *initiation*?

Now, initiation comes from the Latin word *initio*, which simply means to make a beginning. An initiation is a beginning, but of a special kind. Initiations are ceremonies which mark the beginning in ritualized form, meant to crystallize the work of the beginning in the consciousness of the initiate.

Notice that most initiation ceremonies actually seem to mark the end of something. A high school graduation ceremony is an initiation, but it comes at the end of high school. Confirmation is an initiation, but it comes at the end of a long course of study and preparation. Receiving a black belt in a martial arts school is an initiation, but everyone who has done this knows that it comes at the end of many years of hard work and training. All initiations have this element of ending, but are also beginnings. The high school graduation marks the beginning of adulthood. Conformation marks the beginning of one's life as a full member of the Church. Receiving a black belt truly marks the beginning of one's work as a martial artist—one teacher I used to have would say, "When you get your black belt is when I see that you're able to learn our system." And so every initiation also, in a way, signifies death and rebirth. At graduation, the child dies and the adult is born. At Confirmation, too, the spiritual child dies, the spiritual adult is born. The black belt martial artist has died to the life of the student and begun the new life of the master; that's why it is customary to bow to a black belt in a traditional martial arts school.

As such, the prototype of all initiation is the Death and Resurrection of Our Lord Jesus Christ.

In this course, we will present a ritual of self-initiation, which will mark the initiate's beginning in the higher works of Christian magic.

Finally, let's talk about *Mystery*.

In this book, I'm going to talk about Christianity as a Mystery religion. As usual, the common definition will give us no help. When we say that Christianity is a Mystery religion, we don't mean that it has something to do with an Agatha Christie novel.

A Mystery religion is a cult built around the myth of a particular God or Goddess. (Please keep in mind that the word "cult" simply means "a specific religious practice," not a group of people who live in a compound, obey a charismatic leader absolutely, and may or may not eventually drink poisoned Kool-Aid.) The God or Goddess in question is usually the sort who dies and rises again. The Mystery religions or Mystery cults were based around rituals of initiation in which the death and rebirth of the deity were re-enacted. Those who experienced the initiation became initiates of the Mystery.

In ancient times, there were Mystery cults built around many of the gods of the ancient world. Osiris, Bacchus, Mithra, Cybele, and Orpheus. The best-known of all the Mysteries was the Mystery of Eleusis, which re-enacted the descent of the goddess Persephone into the Underworld and her marriage to Hades, the god of Death. In ancient times, some of the Mysteries admitted men only; others were for women; and still others, including Eleusis, admitted men and women both. Mysteries such as those of Eleusis were one-time events; one went through the initiation once, and passed from being a novice to an initiate. Others, including the cult of Mithras, were based on a graded sequence of initiation. Mithras's cult was especially popular among Roman soldiers, who built underground temples called mithraea all over the Roman world. In the initiations of Mithras, there were seven grades of initiation. One passed in sequence from the grades of Raven, to the grade of occult, and then the grades of Soldier, Lion, Persian, Runner of the Sun, and Father. Among other things, initiates of the Mysteries were known to lose their fear of death.

It's easy to see the connection to traditional Christianity. The seven Sacraments are all rituals of High Magic. Some, of course, are performed only once, and these are particularly called rituals of initiation. The Sacraments of Confession and Communion are performed regularly, but they have an initiatory aspect to them as well. Confession is a purification of the soul, which is followed by a Communion with the Divine that has its proper effect only when the soul has been purified.

It's important to note that, although many people attend Mass and receive Communion weekly, the Catholic Church obliges its members to receive Communion only once per year, and that this should take place at Eastertime. This mirrors the once-yearly performance of the Eleusinian and other Mystery rituals in ancient times. Interestingly, the tradition of a yearly Communion evolved during the Middle Ages, as though the ancient pattern were simply lying in wait in the collective unconscious, slowly reasserting itself.

The next few concepts are simpler.

> **Exoteric and esoteric.** The term "exoteric" refers to the public practices and teachings of the mainstream Christian churches. In the context of this book, "mainstream churches" are specifically the Sacramental churches: that is, the Roman Catholic, the Anglican, and to a certain extent the Lutheran. The term "esoteric" refers to the inner meaning of the public practices and teachings. Esoteric ideas are hidden, sometimes in plain sight, and are sometimes kept secret from the public. "Esoteric Christianity," is that Christian tradition which is based on the inner or hidden side of the Christian religion.
>
> This is a work of Esoteric Christianity, but it's important to understand precisely what that means. It was common, at one time, to present esoteric ideas as though they were part of a secret tradition handed down from one initiate to another from early times, often from Jesus himself. This was probably never true, and it certainly is not true today. The esoteric ideas which are presented in this book were learned by its author in a much more prosaic fashion: through the study of old texts, membership in initiatory orders, and talking with well-informed people. Moreover, this book differs from other esoteric works in that it does not rely on Gnostic texts or lost Gospels. The practices herein are derived from the traditions of European Christendom and its descendant cultures

in North America, and the readings come entirely from the Bible and the canonical Gospels, with one exception.

That exception is *The Gospel of Nicodemus*, which is the source of the tradition of the Harrowing of Hell. You should know, however, that though *The Gospel of Nicodemus* is not canonical, it is also not heretical. It is one of those texts which, at one time, were not read in church but which provided inspiration and understanding for the Church. The tradition of the Harrowing of Hell is not emphasized today, but it was in earlier times; Dante references it in the *Inferno*, for example.

Occult. From time to time, the word "occult" is used in this book, though I have minimized it in order to avoid confusion. Today, people often, incorrectly, associate it with devil worship and evil magic. In reality, "occult" simply means "hidden," and is a synonym for "esoteric." A student or practitioner of "the occult" is an "occultist." Again, please note, that does not mean "a devil worshiper."

Egregore. The term "egregore" is used by occultists to refer to the collective mind that emerges any time a group of human beings come together. Families, churches, towns, and even subcultures from football fans to punk rockers have egregores.

The Planes. The planes are levels of being. This means that they refer to different types of existence. These different types, moreover, are related in a hierarchical fashion. The first plane is the plane of unity, also called the Henadic plane or the Divine Plane. It is the realm of unity from which all things emerge and is associated with God the Father and with the varying names of God found in the Old Testament and in such theological works as the *Divine Names* of St. Dionysius the Areopagite. The second plane is the plane of mind, also called the Divine Mind and the Intellectual or Noetic Plane. The second plane is the plane of the Ideas, which are the archetypal forms of the things that exist in our world. It is associated with Christ and is also the habitation of angels and saints. The third plane is the plane of the soul, also called the Psychic or Astral Plane. It includes most ordinary thinking, imagination, and emotions. It is associated with both the Holy Spirit and the Devil and is the natural habitation of spirits, both good and evil. The fourth plane is the plane of energy, called the Etheric or Energetic Plane. It is the source of the life energy which animates all living beings. It is associated with nature and the Moon, and also with the substance or pseudo-substance that goes under the name of qi, ki, prana, ruach, pneuma, or spiritus in Chinese, Japanese, Sanskrit, Hebrew, Greek, and Latin, respectively. The final plane is the Material or Physical Plane. This is the realm of natural bodies which we encounter with our senses.

It's important to note that, while the three highest planes are associated with the three persons of the Holy Trinity, the Holy Trinity are not limited to those planes, and they are not separate from one another. Rather, the Trinity as a whole exists in an eternal unity, unimaginable to the human mind and beyond even the Divine Plane.

Below the Physical Plane is Chaos, which is also matter without form. This is distinct from the matter which we encounter, which always has form, shape, and substance.

In the esoteric tradition, we understand that the work of the spiritual life consists of "rising on the planes," that is, raising the level of our consciousness from the material senses, through the Astral and to the Mental or Intellectual plane. There is an opposing current, however, which seeks to drag us downward, involving us in the lower part of the Astral Plane, which is the source of painful emotions and controlling desires, and down still further into the purely sensory realm of the Material, and even into the unformed Chaos below. "Imprisonment in matter" is the condition in which consciousness is trapped in sensation and in the impulses of the Lower Astral; this is what the exoteric traditions call the state of sin. Sin itself is that force which seeks to drive us downward.

A note on translations

It is customary in a work like this to choose a single translation of the Bible when presenting Scriptural passages. I have chosen to forgo this custom. Readings from Genesis are taken from the King James translation, while passages from the Gospels are taken from the Douay-Rheims version. Both of these are old translations of the Bible, and that helps us in our work because they are connected with well-established energetic currents. The King James Bible, moreover, has a long tradition of use in magic in the English-speaking world.

The selection from *The Gospel of Nicodemus* in the chapter on Holy Saturday is from *The Lost Books of the Bible*, edited by Rutherford H. Platt, Jr., 1926.

A note on seasonal symbolism

Much of the material in this book relates to the natural world and the cycle of the seasons. In the Northern Hemisphere, of course, Easter is a Spring holiday, and much of its symbolism and associated traditions derive from that fact. If you happen to be located in the Southern Hemisphere, you will have to modify some of the practices accordingly.

Getting started

In order to get the most out of this book and these practices, you're going to need a few tools. If you've worked through the previous books in this series, you will already have most of the material you need.

> **A working space.** The first thing you need is simply a space in which to do the work. Some people set aside an entire room in their homes for magical practice, but this isn't necessary (and most of us don't have enough space!). A corner of your bedroom where you can remain undisturbed for up to an hour is enough.
>
> **An altar.** This is a small table or other flat surface which provides a focus for prayer and meditation. It can be as simple as a folding TV tray, which can be taken down after your work is complete, or even the top of a dresser or end table. Alternatively, it can be as elaborate as a fixed altar in a corner of your home. The rest of the tools indicated are all placed on your altar, so make sure that, whatever you are
>
> **A crucifix.** You will need a crucifix for your altar, and it's best if it is one that can stand on its own. These can be purchased for relatively little cost at Catholic supply stores or online.
>
> **A container for holy water.** This can be a cup or small bowl, and, again, may be as simple or as ornate as your taste and your budget permit.

A container for incense. There are different ways to do this. An incense holder for stick incense works, and you can also fill a small cup with sand and place an incense stick upright in it. If you prefer resin incense, you can use a thurible; note that these require charcoal.

Candles. You should have at least one candle burning on your altar, and you may prefer two or three. (Don't go overboard, and make sure to use common sense when working with open flame.) You will also need one additional candle, which should be solid white. This will be lit on Holy Saturday.

Other sacred items. Beyond this, your altar can contain whatever other sacred items or decorations you like. At minimum, an image or statue of the Virgin Mary is highly recommended, and you can also include images of whatever other saints or angels you work with.

Altar cloths. You will need to cover your altar or altar space with a cloth. This can be a small piece of fabric of a single color; these are easily found at craft stores and online. Certain colors have a symbolic role in Western liturgies, and these are seen in the colors worn by the priests and deacons on different occasions. We are going to make use of this color symbolism in our work by using altar cloths of different colors depending on the day.

The specific colors you will need are:

> **Green.** Green is the color of nature and life, and, in the Catholic tradition, is the color used at Mass during ordinary time. We will use a green altar cloth during the short season of pre-Lent or Gesimatide, which precedes Ash Wednesday. Traditionally, violet was used during this season, but the shift from green to violet on Ash Wednesday will allow us to symbolize the change in the seasonal energy and help produce the necessary shift in our own consciousness.
>
> **Violet.** Violet (or purple) is a symbol of mourning and repentance, as we saw at Advent. It is used throughout the Lenten season, with one exception.

Rose. Rose (or pink) is a symbol of joy. It is used two times during the year: At Gaudete Sunday in Advent and at Laetare Sunday, which is the Fourth Sunday in Lent.

White. This symbolizes purity and the powers of Heaven. It is used on Easter Sunday, and from there forward until Pentecost.

Yellow. Yellow (or gold), in the esoteric tradition, specifically symbolizes the element of Air. We will use it exclusively during the Spring Ember Days.

Red. Red symbolizes at once the fire of divine love and the blood of Christ. It is used extensively in the contemporary Church, but for the purpose of this book we are only going to make use of it once, at Pentecost.

A Bible. Throughout Lent, we are going to read certain passages from the Christian Scriptures. In most cases, these are provided for you, but in some cases they are prohibitively long, incorporating entire chapters from the various Gospels. In those cases, the correct readings are indicated, and you will have to find them yourself. The Gospel translations presented are from the Douay-Rheims version, but you can use another translation if you like, with certain caveats. The New International Version is best avoided, and other translations of the Bible which seek to render it in "modern language," such as the Message Bible, are very bad. In addition to the Douay-Rheims, the King James Bible and the Revised Standard Edition are best.

A journal and pen. The final thing that you will need is a journal. The form of meditation that we will practice in this book makes use of the thinking mind, rather than silencing it as in some forms of meditation. Because of this, you will find it very helpful to have a pen and a notebook on hand, in order to write down the ideas that come to you.

CHAPTER TWO

The foundations of Christian magic

This section introduces the fundamental concepts of this book. We begin by providing a set of instructions in the foundational practices of the system of Sacramental Magic. These are found in the other books in this series, so if you've read those, this section will be a review. If you are new to this work, however, you will want to pay close attention to this part. We then continue with a brief overview of the seasons of Lent and Easter, discussing both their history and associated traditions and beginning to introduce some elements of the esoteric approach to this time of year. Finally, we discuss the season of Gesimatide or pre-Lent, the short season which precedes Lent itself. During Gesimatide, we begin the work that will conclude many months from now, at Pentecost.

In order to get the most out of this book, there are certain practices that you will need to commit to performing every day. In the previous book on Christmas, I presented these practices one at a time over the weeks of Advent. In this book, I'm going to present them all at once. If you've read either *The Book of Sacramental Magic* or the *Sacramental Magic of Advent*, you already know how to do all of these, and you can either skip this section or treat it as a refresher course. If you're new to this material I'd encourage you to read this section carefully, and then incorporate each practice one at a time. That is to say, you should work with each practice by itself for as long as you feel you need to in order to "get it" before you add in the next one. The practices build on one another, and you should learn them in the order presented.

Please note: This section is entitled "Foundations of Practice," because these are basic, daily practices. They are suitable for all times and all seasons. If you pick up this book in late September, with Easter half a year away, you can begin these practices now. They will benefit you immensely.

There are other practices which we will discuss, which are specific to the seasons of Lent and Easter. These include the practices of fasting and almsgiving during Lent, and special meditations on specific holy days and feasts. Those practice will gain strength from building on the foundation of these daily practices. To give an analogy, the daily practices are akin to a musician working with scales and chord progressions on a daily basis, while the special practices are more like an actual concert performance.

Foundational practice 1: A prayer rule

This shouldn't need to be said, but prayer is not an optional practice in the life of a Christian, and that includes a Christian magician. Fortunately, the Catholic tradition includes an enormous treasury of prayers. If you do not already have a daily prayer rule, now is the time to develop one.

A simple rule is to say the Our Father; three Hail Marys; and the Glory Be each morning, as early as possible. This connects with the Rosary, which begins with these prayers. If you like, you can extend this practice by the use of the Angelus, which is included in the appendixes at the back of this book. After this, you can either sit in silence for a moment, or pray to specific saints with whom you have a relationship. If you don't have a relationship with any saints, this is a good time to get acquainted with them. If you don't know where to begin, start with your own guardian angel and your patron saint (or the saint for whom you are named).

If another prayer rule appeals to you or you already have your own practice, you may make use of that instead.

If you are completely new to this kind of work, a simple prayer rule will be enough for a week or two. Once you've established the habit, move on to the next section, which covers the Banishing Sign of the Cross. This is a specific way of working with the traditional Sign of the Cross that enhances its magical effects. Please note: Once you begin, you will perform the Banishing Sign of the Cross *before* your daily prayer rule, not after.

Foundational practice 2: Banishing

Most modern magical traditions are built around a banishing ritual. These rituals have three purposes, which are carried out simultaneously: First, they connect the practitioner of the ritual with the highest form of the divine as conceived in their particular tradition. Second, they clear the working space and the mind and aura of the magician, in preparation for deeper forms of magic and meditation. Third, in their symbolism, they contain, in condensed form, the entire symbolic structure of their particular tradition. The best-known and most widely practiced of contemporary banishing rituals is the Golden Dawn's Lesser Banishing Ritual of the Pentagram; others include the Star Ruby of the Thelema tradition, the Sphere of Protection, especially, among modern Druid orders, and the Wiccan practice of casting a circle and calling the quarters.

Of course, most of these will not do for our purposes—at least, not in the forms in which they're currently practiced. (There are a few exceptions, which will be detailed below.) Fortunately, Christianity has its own banishing ritual, profoundly simple, and yet noted for thousands of years for its effectiveness. This ritual, of course, is the *Sign of the Cross*.

In our tradition, we perform the Sign of the Cross before prayer and meditation, just as your grandmother does. The only difference is that we make use of some of the techniques developed by the larger magical tradition in order to enhance the power of the Sign of the Cross as a banishing ritual. Three techniques in particular provide the foundation for our work. Let's take a moment to discuss them, and then we'll proceed to practical instructions for the Sign of the Cross. They are:

1. **Visualization.** Everyone knows that visualization, or deliberate imagination, has magical power. If you don't know this, it's easy enough to prove it to yourself. Take a moment to scan your body from head to toe. Notice your posture; the muscles of your head and face; any places you are holding tension; any sensations of pain or

electrical vibration. Notice your emotional state, and take a moment to consider what sorts of feelings or thoughts have been playing out in your mind for the last hour or so. Then, close your eyes and imagine, as vividly as you can, a peaceful forest in early Spring. Feel the warmth of the air, and a gentle breeze on your face; hear the birds, singing in the trees; smell the air, and take in the scent of flowers and new leaves. Focus on this scene for a minute or two. Then let the scene go, and scan your body again. Now, what do you notice?

In our work, we make use of this power of visualization in order to bring about changes in our state of consciousness. This is already magic, and for some people, it will be enough to think of our work in this way. You should know, however, that according to contemporary magical theory, *visualization* or *active imagination* allows us to influence the Astral Plane within ourselves and our surrounding environment.

2. **Vibration.** This is a simple but very effective magical technique. Vibration consists of singing or chanting a word in such a way that you feel a noticeable buzz or vibration in a certain part of the body. Some people find that this comes very easily, while others struggle with it. If you are in the latter category, when you come across instructions to "vibrate" a word, simply sing or chant it and *imagine* that you feel a vibration in the area indicated.

3. **Sacred language.** We will be making use of Latin in our basic ritual. This is the sacred language of the Roman Catholic Church, and its use should never have been abandoned. Making use of it allows us to connect with the larger psychic current or *egregore* of the Catholic tradition. If you don't know Latin yourself, by the way, don't worry: The unfamiliarity of the language can actually aid in your magical work, by circumventing your rational, thinking mind and getting directly to the higher mind.

The banishing sign of the cross: Practical instructions

Step 1. Imagine a brilliant point of light located at an infinite distance above your head. Know that this light is not God the Father, but is, rather, the closest that a human mind can come to comprehending the power of God the Father.

Step 2. Now, imagine a column of light descending from that remote point down through the cosmos, finally coming to rest at the crown of your head. Reach up with your right hand, and draw the light to your forehead. Vibrate the words *IN NOMINE PATRIS*. The vibration should be felt at the forehead.

Step 3. Draw your hand to your heart. As you do, bow your head, and imagine the column of light descending down, through the centerline of your body, and all the way into the heart of the Earth. Vibrate *ET FÍLII*. The vibration should be felt through the entire centerline of the body.

Step 4. Draw your hand up and out to your left shoulder, and then your right shoulder. As you do so, visualize another line of white light rising up from the heart of the Earth, meeting the first at your heart, and then extending outward to either direction in infinite space. Vibrate *ET SPIRITU SANCTI*.

Step 5. Bring both of your hands together at your heart. Imagine a sphere of golden light at your heart. Vibrate the word Amen, feeling the word at the heart. As you do so, imagine that sphere expanding outward in every direction, until it surrounds you on all sides. Know that you are surrounded and protected by the Light Divine.

You can now proceed to your work of daily prayer and meditation, which will be discussed below.

After your meditations, make the Sign of the Cross again. This time, though, you can do so more quickly, closer to the way that people ordinarily do—though you should always pray with a reverent attitude. You will find, even if you rush through it, you will re-connect to the energy of the fuller ritual, so that any time you make the Sign of the Cross in daily life, it will have an added power and majesty.

Note: There are, as mentioned above, a few banishing rituals from other traditions which are equally suitable to our work. These include any rituals which are explicitly Christian and use Christian symbolism. The Sphere of Protection is one example: This is a ritual which allows practitioners to invoke whatever powers or gods they personally work with. A Sphere of Protection which invoked Odin and Freya or Zeus and Hera would, obviously, not work, but one which invoked the Holy Trinity and the angels that govern the Four Elements would be fine. Equally, the modified version of the Golden Dawn's pentagram created by A.E. Waite, which uses the cross instead of the star in the quarters, would also be acceptable. It is possible that the pentagram ritual used in the Golden Dawn tradition would work, since the divine names are drawn entirely from the Old Testament—though this is a matter for experimentation. If in doubt (or if none of this material is familiar to you), simply use the ritual as given; it works just fine.

Foundational practice 3: Lectio divina

Like prayer, meditation is not optional in our work. In recent years, various forms of meditation have become popular throughout the Western world, mostly rooted in the traditions of India and China. This is, by and large, a good thing, and even a very good thing. The only trouble is that certain meditation practices have often been cut off from their roots in a larger tradition, including complementary practices that are intended to go together. The Western world has its own meditative traditions, and we will be making use of these, as they work well with the practices given in this book. The specific form of meditation that we will be practicing is called *lectio divina*, or divine reading.

Lectio divina is a specific way of approaching sacred texts that allows us to make use of the full powers of the mind and the spirit. It's worth noting that we can apply *lectio divina* to *any* text at all. In this book, we will be working with specific passages from Scripture as well as certain other texts which will be presented. Once you've made your way through this book, however, you can make use of it with any text you like, including texts outside the Christian tradition. The dialogues of Plato, to give one example, are very amenable to *lectio divina*. So are classical legends and myths from the *Odyssey* of Homer to the *Divine Comedy* of Dante Alighieri and religious texts from other traditions, such as the *Daodejing* and the *Baghavad Gita*.

If you currently practice mindfulness meditation, zazen, or a similar Eastern practice, by the way, there is no need to give it up in order to work with this book. You may, however, need to move it to a different time of the day. And, to get the most out of this book you will need to add in the meditative work which we will describe.

Lectio divina: *Practical instructions*

Step 1. Perform the Banishing Sign of the Cross, and whatever prayer rule you have adopted (the sequence of the Our Father, three Hail Marys, and the Glory Be will do nicely).

Step 2. Read the passage indicated.

Step 3. Sit in a comfortable posture, with your back straight, and close your eyes. Take a few minutes to breathe rhythmically, in order to relax your energetic body. If you are unfamiliar with rhythmic breathing, a simple method is to inhale slowly for a count of four; retain the breath for a count of four; exhale for a count of four, and hold the lungs empty for a count of four. This is called the fourfold breath. It is also used by singers, in order to expand the lungs, and by first responders, in order to calm the mind to respond to challenging events. It will work for you, too.

Step 4. Bring to mind the passage that you have read. (You can re-read it if you need to.) Allow yourself to turn it over, and to think about it. Eventually, something specific will jump out at you. You may find yourself visualizing the scene in active imagination, from the perspective of one of the characters. Follow this, and see where it takes you. Alternatively, you may find yourself thinking discursively about an idea or a concept within the text, with no visual components to your thought at all. This works just as well. The point is to follow a specific theme for a set period of time—five to ten minutes is good to start.

Step 5. Release your meditation, and turn your attention to God. Take a moment to pray on whatever topic seemed most important during your meditation. The form your prayer takes is up to you. It may be a request that you be aided in developing one of the virtues—the courage of Christ as he waited at Gethsemane, for example, or the faith of the good thief on the cross at Calvary. It may be an expression of gratitude to God for one of his gifts. It may be that your mind is turned toward one of the saints found in the Passion narratives, such as Mary Magdalene, Longinus the Centurion, Saint John, or Our Lady. All of these different approaches are acceptable.

Step 6. Finally, take a moment to release all discursive thought and simply sit in quiet contemplation for a time. Be aware of the presence and power of God, of His gifts to us as they were presented to you in your meditation, the presence and intercessory power of His saints. You can keep your mind still by returning to rhythmic breathing through the fourfold breath or whatever method you prefer.

Step 7. Slowly open your eyes and rise to your feet. You can say a short prayer to close your meditation. This can either be an extemporaneous or a liturgical prayer, such as the Fatima Prayer, the Prayer of Saint Francis, or the Holy Spirit Prayer, all of which can be found in the back of this book. Always conclude with the Sign of the Cross.

Foundational practice 4: Opening a magical temple

On an everyday basis, the practices just given will usually be more than enough. They can also be performed anywhere—kneeling at the edge of your bed, seated on your couch next to your morning coffee, or even on public transportation.

Sometimes, however, we want to go deeper with the work, and for that we're going to need to set aside a special place, which will require more involved ritual work. We usually call this a magical temple, though if that idea makes you uncomfortable for whatever reason you can simply think of it as a working space. Don't imagine that you need to set aside an entire room for this sort of work if you don't have it, by the way. A corner of your living room or bedroom will do just fine, and it doesn't need to be used exclusively for magic. In a worst-case scenario you can sit on the edge of your bed and use the top of your dresser as an altar. The rule is always "Do what you can with what you have."

A magical temple or working space will need a few additional pieces of equipment. Specifically, you will need:

1. **An altar.** Ideally, this is a permanent space on which you can place religious objects such as a crucifix, statues of the saints, holy water, and so on. For many people, setting aside a permanent altar isn't practical, and so in practice it can be any flat surface. A folding TV tray will do, provided it's stable enough that you don't have to worry about it tipping over; so will the top of a desk or a dresser.
2. **Altar cloths.** These will vary in color depending on the day, as described above.
3. **A container of holy water.** If you don't have holy water, you can usually get it from any local Catholic or Orthodox church, and you can even order it online. You can also make it yourself; detailed instructions are given in The Book of Sacramental Magic.
4. **Incense.** These days many people have a hard time tolerating incense. I always find this somewhat odd, since the same people seem to have no problem with harsh chemical cleaners and "air fresheners." With that said, there are right and wrong ways to use incense in the home, and at the back of this book you'll find a simple guide to using incense that should minimize the likelihood of a reaction.

5. **A candle.** This should, ideally, be pure white. Candles with holy images and prayers in good Spanish and bad English can easily be found in most grocery stores these days.
6. **Additional sacred items.** This is mostly up to you. At a minimum, you should have a statue or holy card depicting the Virgin Mary. Beyond that, you can also include statues or images of your own patron saints and other saints you are working with; additional prayer candles; a Bible; prayer books; flowers; and anything else you like.
7. **A chair or stool for meditation.** This should have a flat surface on which you can sit up straight with your feet flat on the floor. If you like, you can also choose to meditate while kneeling, and you can make use of a kneeler (these can be purchased for the home, though they're somewhat expensive); a pad or mat; or the type of meditation bench common in Eastern traditions.

The opening ritual

Step 1. Enter your temple or magical working space and sit quietly for a minute or two, clearing your mind of the day thus far. When you feel ready, rise and light the candle on your altar.

Step 2. Perform the Banishing Sign of the Cross, exactly as instructed above.

Step 3. Take the holy water from the altar and hold it up over your head (or at least at eye level). Say the words:

> Thou shalt cleanse me with hyssop, Oh Lord, and I shall be clean. Thou shalt wash me, and I shall be whiter than snow. Have mercy on me, Oh Lord, according to Thy great mercy.

Flick the water three times (once for Father, Son, and Holy Spirit) to each quarter of the room or working space. As you do so, imagine that the holy water is creating a kind of bubble around your space, driving out any stray thoughts or unbalancing energies that remained after your banishing ritual.

Step 4. Trace the Sign of the Cross over the incense, and as you do so say the words:

> Be thou blessed by Him in Whose honor thou shalt be burned.

Then light the incense, and say:

> May this incense, blessed by Thee, Oh Lord, ascend to Thee; and may Thy mercy descend upon us.

Pick up the incense (either in its container or by itself if it's an incense stick), trace the Sign of the Cross at each of the four corners of the room or working space. As you do so, imagine that the energies of the Divine descend into the room in which you are working. If you're working with incense in a stick or another form easily doused, you can extinguish it at this point.

Step 5. Stand in front of your altar, and hold your hands out in front of you with the palms turned up. This is called the *orans* posture, and we will continue to make use of it as we go. Say the word:

> Our help is in the Name of the Lord, who hath made the Heavens and the Earth.
> Be with me, Oh Lord, and guide me in the work I am about to perform.
> Amen.

This completes the Opening.

Once you have completed your intended work, perform the following ritual to close the temple.

The closing ritual

Step 1. Stand with your hands in the orans posture, and say the following words:

> May this work, which I have performed this day, be blessed by Almighty God, and may the Holy Spirit guide its effects in accordance with Divine Law. I thank thee, Oh God Almighty, [if you have been working with a specific saint, say, "And thee, blessed Saint. N.," and all of you holy angels and saints for your assistance in this work. In the Name of Jesus Christ, our Lord, let all spirits depart from this place in peace, and let there be peace between us.

Step 2. Repeat the asperges with holy water.

Step 3. Repeat the censing with incense.

Step 4. Trace the Sign of the Cross over your altar, and say a closing prayer. This is a prayer of devotion—that is, not a prayer asking for a specific intercession—that serves to create a sense of connection to God. Which prayer you choose is up to you, as some will be more suitable for different occasions. Good choices include the Prayer of Saint Francis, the Fatima Prayer, and the Glory Be, all of which can be found in the appendixes to this book. Then say the following words:

> In the name of the Father, and of the Son, and of the Holy Spirit,
> I now proclaim this temple closed.

CHAPTER THREE

An overview of the seasons of Lent and Easter

Easter, as noted above, is the most important, indeed, the central holiday in the Christian religion. As a great feast, it is preceded by a great fast. And this great fast is Lent, which is considerably longer and more rigorous than the Advent fast.

The history of Lent

The Lenten Fast dates back at least to the fourth century, and it was preceded in times still earlier by shorter fasting periods.

Lent is, in theory, a 40-day fast, though the actual length of time between its beginning and Easter Sunday is 46 days. This is because the six Sundays aren't counted. Sunday is the Lord's day, and so every Sunday is a kind of Easter; for this reason, fasting on this day is considered inappropriate. (As we will see, whether or not this applies to us depends very much on the type of fast we choose to undertake.) We will have more to say about the nature of the Lenten Sundays later on in this chapter.

Lent's nature as a 40-day fast is reflected in its name in many languages. In Latin it is *Quadragesima*, meaning "40th," and the Spanish *Cuaresma* and Italian *Quaresima* are derived from that. The English word

"Lent" comes from an Anglo-Saxon word, *lencten*, which referred to the "lengthening" of the day in Springtime. This, in turn, reflects the way that many pre-Christian seasonal festivals have been baptized and built upon by the Christian church.

Lent is preceded by a brief season known as Gesimatide or pre-Lent. This begins on Septuagesima, three Sundays prior to Ash Wednesday. In the modern Catholic Church, this season has been suppressed, but (like many of the things they have suppressed) it is well worth reviving, particularly in our private practice. Gesimatide was historically both a time to prepare for the rigorous fast of Lent and a Carnival season. We will discuss Gesimatide in greater detail in a future chapter.

Lent is a fast, and many of the traditions associated with it are specific types of fasting foods. The pretzel began its origin as a Lenten fasting bread, originally made only from flour, water, and salt. (It is worth noting, as an aside, that in earlier times flours were much heartier than those used in most modern baking, and thus subsisting on pretzels was a far more sustainable option.) Though most are unaware of the popular snacks' origin, they retain their original shape, which resembles two arms crossed in prayer.

There are numerous other traditional Lenten foods; indeed, most Christian countries got around to inventing at least one. In England, this took the form of hot cross buns. Their origin is remembered in an old version of their anthem (only a few of the world's confections have been so lucky as to get their own anthem):

> Good Friday comes this month, the old woman runs,
> With one a penny, two a penny, hot cross buns,
> Whose virtue is, if you believe what's said,
> They'll not grow mouldy like the common bread.

Other common Lenten foods include such appealing dishes as the Polish *zur*, a type of mush made of rye; and soups consisting of beans, lentils, or split peas along with some spices and vegetables. These latter sorts of dishes can be easily re-created in the modern home, and provide much more nourishing faire than pretzels.

Doppelbock, a type of strong (and very tasty) beer, is supposed to have been invented by monks of the Paulaner order, who were not allowed to eat solid food during Lent. There are some sources which dispute this, and I personally can't see how it would be possible: doppelbock is high in calories, sure, but it's also very high in alcohol, and I suspect 40 straight days of it would produce little more than a brutal hangover. On the other hand, before the German beer purity law of 1516, it was common for beer to be brewed using a variety of herbs besides hops, which are the primary flavoring ingredient used in beer today. Some of these were mildly, or even quite strongly psychoactive, and it's amusing to imagine supposedly grim and austere monks undertaking a 40-day spiritual retreat on a diet of booze and psychedelics.

All joking (and booze) aside, Lent is primarily a penitential season, and its customs reflect this. Lenten foods are simple and flavorless, the point being simply to sustain the body, and not to delight the senses. Confession and acts of public penitence have always marked this time of year. In many Catholic countries, Lent is marked by solemn processions and even by public acts of mortification.

In the Western world, Easter always falls on the First Sunday, after the first Full Moon, after the Spring Equinox. This dating method has an important astrological significance, which we will discuss later.

Like Christmas, the Easter feast was not, historically, limited to a single day. Rather, the feasting and celebration continued through the week that followed, and additional feast days followed Easter itself.

The Easter season culminates in the days of the Ascension and Pentecost. Ascension celebrates the Ascension of Jesus into Heaven. Following this are ten days which conclude with Pentecost, which celebrates the descent of the Holy Spirit onto the Disciples in the Upper Room. Our work in this book concludes with Pentecost and includes special meditations for both Pentecost and Ascension.

The structure of Lent and Easter

From Ash Wednesday to Easter Sunday, there are 46 days, of which six are Sundays. We describe Lent as a 40-day fast, but this is really "40 days, not including Sunday." There is a special reason for this, and it's not simply that we like Sunday. Sunday, according to the ancient tradition, is the day of the Sun. It is also the day of our Lord's Resurrection. This sets Sunday aside and makes it special: In a certain sense, it is outside of time. In another sense, as the day of the Sun, the star which gives life to the Earth and by which we judge the day and the night, it is a stand-in for Time itself. In the Bible, the concept of the "day" is a symbol for Time as a whole and for an Age of time. We see this right from the beginning, in the Book of Genesis, when the Lord is said to have created the Earth and all its inhabitants "in six days." Each of these days is symbolic, both of an age and of a level of reality.

And so all Sundays are symbols both of the Creation of the world and of its Redemption, which is really a Second Creation. It is very fitting, from this perspective, that there are six Sundays in Lent, and that the seventh is Easter itself. The six Sundays represent the six days of Creation, and the seventh Sunday represents the day on which the Lord rested. That Seventh Day was not simply God taking a break: It really refers to God establishing Himself on the throne of the Heavens. In a certain sense, the historical Easter, when the man Jesus of Nazareth was executed, descended into Hell, and returned again to Earth, truly *is* the Seventh Day of Creation, on which the Lord established His dominion throughout the Universe, from the heights to the depths.

Notice that Advent, which begins the liturgical year, relates to the end of the world and the Second Coming, while Lent, which follows it, symbolizes the Creation. This apparent reversal of time, in which the end precedes the beginning, is no accident. It reflects, instead, a secret teaching which lies hidden in the Christian tradition. See if you can figure out what it is.

In the chapters which follow, we will explore the symbolism of Lent and Easter as an image of the Seven Days of Creation, in addition to their usual symbolism in Christian practice.

Following Lent, there is a second set of Seven Sundays. These seven begin with Low Sunday, the First Sunday after Easter, and end with Pentecost, when the Holy Spirit descends upon the Disciples in the Upper Room. This represents a kind of Second Creation, which is also the return of the original Creation to the Creator. During the first Creation, God brings the world and all its inhabitants into being. During the Second Creation, the Universe is gathered back into God. This is represented by the "descent of the Holy Spirit" at Pentecost. The Holy Spirit, being God, doesn't *really* go anywhere: instead, the Disciples ascend to *Him*, and are divinized. This is a representation of the completion of the journey of all created beings, who have their origin in the Mind of God, descend into material incarnation, and return again to the Father.

The two sets of Seven Sundays form a process of initiation. This is the true initiation into the inner side of the Christian tradition, Christianity as a Mystery religion. This cycle will provide the structure for our work as we continue.

Gesimatide

The weeks leading up to Lent are known as *Gesimatide*. This odd name refers to the names of the three Sundays prior to Ash Wednesday. The first of the three is called Septuagesima, the second is Sexagesima, and the Sunday immediately before Ash Wednesday is called Quinquegesima. These names, as you might have guessed, come from Latin: *Septuagesima* means "70th"; *Sexagesima* means "60th"; and *Quinquagesima* means "50th." You should probably know that Septuagesima, Sexagesima, and Quinquagesima are not actually the 70th, 60th, and 50th days before Lent—any more than Lent actually lasts for 40 days.

Gesimatide has two traditional purposes. It could be said that one of these purposes is sacred, the other secular, but the truth is that both are intertwined during Gesimatide. On the one hand, this season is known as "pre-Lent," and it is a time of preparation for the coming season of fasting and abstinence. In the secular world, however, it has a long history as a carnival season.

Gesimatide, then, can see it as a season in which the sacred and secular, the joyous and the penitential, intertwine. At the beginning of Lent, we will separate these two elements. Lent focuses on penitence, and Easter and Paschaltide on joy and celebration. The two ideas then come back together at the conclusion of the season at Pentecost. Readers familiar with traditional alchemy will already have recognized the process being described here. The motto of the old alchemists was *Solve et coagula*, or "Separate and combine." In the alchemy of minerals and herbs, material substances are broken down into their constituent components, purified, and recombined in such a way that their higher, spiritual natures express themselves more fully. The work we are doing in this book can also be seen, then, as a kind of spiritual alchemy. This is one of the ways in which the process of initiation works.

And so we begin with Septuagesima, the 70th day before Easter. In the United States and other Protestant-dominated countries, the traditions of Septuagesima have long been abandoned, while the modern Roman Catholic Church, in its hurry to imitate the secular world, has suppressed the season. It nevertheless remains of great value to us, as we prepare for our Lenten pilgrimage.

We will get the most out of Lent if we have already established a foundation of spiritual practice, and Gesimatide provides an excellent opportunity to do that. There are a number of basic practices which are central both to the magical life in general and to the specific work of Lent and Easter.

If you already have one of the previous books in this series, you will already know how to do most of these. If that's the case, don't feel that you need to start over. Simply continue your practices before, and use the Gesima season as an opportunity to re-commit to your daily work.

On the other hand, you may have purchased this book after the beginning of Gesimatide. If that's the case, don't worry. Wherever you are in the course of the Lenten journey is not too late to start. Just learn the practices one by one, at your own pace. All of these practices are meant to form a part of daily work during any season, year after year. If you begin to learn them three weeks after Easter, you'll benefit just as much, and you can focus on the specifically Lenten work next year. Never let excuses keep you from getting started.

Septuagesima

Septuagesima is where our journey begins, three Sundays before Ash Wednesday. Traditionally, this was the last day during which the Alleluia was heard during the Mass; it will not be sung again until Easter.

During Matins, the morning prayer of the Church, the readings for Septuagesima traditionally came from the Book of Genesis. There is an important symbolism here. During the time of Lent and Easter, the world is re-created. Christ, the Divine Mind, in whom are the archetypes of all the things which exist in the world, has himself come into the world as one being among other beings. At His Death on the Cross, he completes the work of Creation itself by descending into the utmost depths of the Universe: that is, into Hell and the World of the Dead, and then returning first to our world, and then to Heaven, to the very seat of the Father. This is a event which occurred in Time around the year 33 AD. Also and more importantly, it is an event which always *is*, outside of Time, in eternity: Christ's power, His providence, and His intellect extend from the source of life and existence in the Father, through the end of the Universe, and return again to the very beginning. This is how the world was renewed, how it is sustained, and how it was created in the first place. And so we begin by reading of the First Creation of the world.

Practice for Septuagesima week

Now is the time to begin to establish a foundation of daily practice. During the course of this book, this practice will expand to include a daily prayer rule, daily banishing, and meditation. Additional practices which are to be performed on a weekly basis will be introduced later on. For now, we can begin with the simplest forms of daily work, which are the daily prayer rule and daily banishing.

Every day this week, starting on Sunday, if you can, perform the Banishing Sign of the Cross. Afterward, take a moment to sit in silence, and then continue with your daily prayer rule. If the task of choosing a prayer rule seems daunting, simply say the Our Father, three Hail Marys, and the Glory Be. It might seem like a lot, especially if you aren't used to this sort of thing, but it shouldn't take more than a few minutes—15 at most, and probably considerably less than that.

This week, you should also begin the work of spiritual reading. As in the case of the daily banishing and prayer, you can choose readings that suit your own practice. At minimum, however, you should read the first chapter of the Book of Genesis, and the Gospel reading from Sunday's Mass. If this is all the spiritual reading you do this week, it will be enough.

We will be working with Genesis extensively over the course of Lent, and now is a good time to familiarize yourself with it.

At Mass on Septuagesima Sunday, the traditional Gospel reading is the Parable of the Laborers in the Vineyard (Matthew 20:1–16). In these verses, if you don't remember, Jesus tells the story of a farmer who went out in the morning to hire laborers to work in his vineyard. Although he hired five groups of workers at five different times, each was paid equally, including those who came in late, "at the eleventh hour." This, we are told, is what the Kingdom of Heaven is like.

The parables of Jesus are very often given simple interpretations, and we often have the impression that our job is to learn the "right" interpretation. Inevitably, this is the interpretation given by some authority, and our "learning" consists only in repetition. Now, it isn't that this form of learning is somehow "wrong." When your child points to an unfamiliar animal and asks its name, you reply "This is a cat" when the child points to a cat, and "This is a dog" when the child points to a dog. When we begin to study our sacred texts, it will be very helpful for us to learn what those who have gone before us have said. If we come to understand no more than this, however, we remain at the level of a child, who learns the names of things but comes to understand nothing on their own. The sacred Scriptures of the Christian tradition, as well as the myths and legends of the saints, are given to us to help us advance in our spiritual lives. In order to truly do so, we need to think about them more deeply and come to our own understanding of what they are saying and why. As you read the Bible passages given this week, take some time to give serious thought to their possible interpretations.

The Septuagesima meditation

The first time you work with this book, you may set this part aside and use the Gesima season to prepare for the more intensive practices of Lent itself. If either this isn't the first time you've done this work, or if you've already familiarized yourself with the work of Sacramental Magic through the previous books in this series, you may practice the following simple Septuagesima meditation.

Preparation. Set up your altar in your temple or working space. The color for today is *green*; the altar should be covered with a green cloth.

Step 1. Open a temple as you have been instructed.

Step 2. Read the Gospel passage cited above, the Parable of the Laborers in the Vineyard from Matthew 20:1–16.

Step 3. Enter into meditation using rhythmic breathing, and visualize and meditate upon the scene you have just read.

Step 4. Rise, and offer the following prayer.

> Late have I come into thy service, O Beauty Ever Ancient,
> Nevertheless, I pray,
> Withhold not from me Thy reward.

Step 5. Close your temple as you have been instructed.

Sexagesima

This is the "60th" day, which means in truth that we have only ten days until Lent begins. It's only a little bit of time, but it will be enough to continue building our foundation of practices.

At this time, you should begin to think seriously about what your Lenten Fast will look like. Take some time to read or re-read the discussion of fasting in the previous part of this book. Think about what might work for you. During your time in prayer, ask the Holy Spirit and your guardian angel to guide you to a fasting regimen suitable for you and your way of life. You might even try one or two possibilities out for a day or two, and see how you feel.

The Gospel reading for Sexagesima Sunday is the Parable of the Sower from the Gospel of Luke 8:4–15. In this story, Jesus describes a farmer who sows his seeds in various places. Some fall upon a path, and are trampled underfoot and eaten by birds. Others fall among rocks, where they sprout but quickly wither. Still others are choked by weeds and die. A few, however, are planted in good soil, where they grow and thrive. Now, as Jesus then tells us, the seeds are the Word of God, and the various soils on which the seeds land represent the dispositions of our own souls, of which some are receptive to the Word, but many are not. As in the case of the Parable of the Laborers, there are layers of meaning in this story far deeper than those immediately apparent.

During Lent, we prepare the soil of our own souls for the reception of the Word, who will be planted in the Earth like a seed on Good Friday, sprout beneath the soil on Holy Saturday and rise again on Easter. All of our Lenten practices are oriented toward this end.

This week, we will begin the work of Christian meditation, which will especially allow us to prepare the soil of our conscious minds to receive the Word of God as revealed in the Scriptures and in other sacred texts.

Practice for Sexagesima

This week, continue the daily banishing and daily prayer rule begun at Septuagesima. (If you did not begin last week, this is the time.) If you feel like you are still "getting the hang of" the banishing, the prayer rule, or simply the idea of daily practice, you can simply stick with that for now. If you feel ready, however, now is the time to begin the work of daily meditation.

Meditation is a critical part of the foundation of any spiritual practice, Christianity included.

The primary form of meditation we will be working with in this book is called *lectio divina*. You will find detailed instructions for the practice of *lectio divina* in Chapter X. If you skipped over that part, now is the time to go back and re-read it. Once you are familiar with the practice of *lectio divina*, you can get started. The same passage may be read more than once, as new ideas will come to you every time.

The best time for *lectio divina* is right after your banishing and prayer. If the demands of your schedule don't allow this, you can separate the two practices if necessary—performing the banishing and prayer in the morning and *lectio divina* at night, say.

The Septuagesima meditation

The first time you work with this book, you may set this part aside, and use the Gesima season to prepare for the more intensive practices of Lent itself. If either this isn't the first time you've done this work, or if you've already familiarized yourself with the work of Sacramental Magic through the previous books in this series, you may practice the following simple Septuagesima meditation.

Preparation. Set up your altar in your temple or working space. The color for today is *green*; the altar should be covered with a green cloth.

Step 1. Open a temple as you have been instructed.

Step 2. Read the Gospel passage cited above, the parable of the sower from Luke (8:4–15).

Step 3. Enter into meditation using rhythmic breathing, and visualize and meditate upon the scene you have just read.

Step 4. Rise, and offer the following prayer.

> Make fertile, oh Lord, the soil of my soul
> That the seed thou plantest there may grow and thrive.

Step 5. Close your temple as you have been instructed.

Quinquagesima

Quinquagesima is also called Cheesefare in Orthodox tradition, as it is on this day that the Eastern Christians bid farewell to dairy products in preparation for Great Lent.

Quinquagesima is also the time of a very wonderful tradition, better kept in the Eastern than in the Western churches, called Forgiveness Sunday. On this day, every member of the church gathers, and each person asks every other person to forgive them for every wrong they have done them during the previous year. This is a powerful way to renew the spirit of a community. From a magical perspective, there are energetic chords, visible on the Astral Plane, which link all the members of a community of any kind to one another, and these chords together form a web which is the collective spirit of the group. Every group of human beings, from churches and families to subcultures and groups of sports fans has such a collective spirit, called an *egregore* by occultists. Now, it happens that egregores can easily corrupt and become degenerate or destructive over time. The practice of collective forgiveness purifies and strengthens the egregore, dissolving chords of resentment and bad behavior and replacing them with chords of mutual support and respect.

Practice for Quinquagesima

Forgiveness Sunday can be practiced by individuals and small groups in two ways.

In the first case, if your circumstances allow it, you can make a focused practiced of forgiveness with your own family. Whether you have a small or large family—even if it's just you and your spouse or partner, or you and your pets—you can set aside a time to ask one another for forgiveness.

You can also do this work on your own, without anyone knowing what you're doing. Take the time to call your friends or family members, or to see them, or to send them a text message, and do the work of taking accountability for your actions that may have harmed them over the last year, and asking their forgiveness. You can tell them about Forgiveness Sunday or not—let the Spirit guide you.

Finally, there is a powerful magical ritual of forgiveness which you can perform. You can make use of this at any time, but you should certainly do so today.

The great forgiveness ritual

Preparation. This ritual is designed to bring forgiveness not to one person alone but to a group of people. It is a modification.

Preparation. You should, by now, have gathered the items necessary to continue our work. Set up a temple or working space as instructed.

The altar should be covered with a green cloth. Make sure to have holy water and a vessel for incense.

Step 1. Begin by performing the Opening Ritual, as described above, in Foundations of Magical Practice.

Step 2. Close your eyes. Say the Lord's Prayer silently to yourself, focusing on the words "forgive us our trespasses, as we forgive those who trespass against us."

Step 3. Bring to mind the person or group you wish to forgive. Try to imagine the situation entirely from the other person's perspective. Imagine what might have led them to do the things they did or to say the things they say. Imagine yourself doing and saying these things. Imagine yourself as the other person (or group, etc.) must see you.

Step 4. Once you feel that you have totally entered into the other party's perspective, and once you are sure you can say this and mean it, silently say: "I understand that you can only be who you are. I forgive you. I forgive you. I forgive you. I am sorry for everything that I did to hurt you, and I hope that you will forgive me."

Step 5. Come out of meditation in the usual way, closing with a suitable prayer and the Sign of the Cross.

It is important that you place no expectations on this practice. The other person may or may not forgive you; their behavior toward you may or may not change. The point is that you have forgiven them. As the Prayer of Saint Francis reminds us, "It is by forgiving that we are forgiven."

Gesimatide and Carnival

Gesimatide, as mentioned above, is the traditional Carnival season. Indeed, the very word "carnival" comes from a Latin phrase, *caro vale*, or "Farewell to meat." Over the course of centuries, the word "carnival" took on its current meaning of a great celebration which extends over many days (or weeks). Unfortunately, this tradition has long been forgotten in much of the English-speaking world. Carnival shared the same fate as most of the great feasts, and the great fasts, being discarded in order to produce a more predictable work week for the sake of industrial production. Thus have we in the modern world come to live far more for the sake of machines than for the sake of men. The exceptions are places like New Orleans, whose cultural foundations are

French rather than English. In places where the Carnival is still kept, it often begins on the Friday of Quinquegesima week and continues until the following Tuesday, which is the last day before Lent. In some places, it lasts even longer, sometimes up to the entire month preceding the beginning of Lent.

It is very difficult to hold a carnival without any other participants and at a time of year when most people are unaware that there is anything to celebrate. This is, therefore, a tradition which can be somewhat difficult to revive. There are a few possibilities, however, which you may find suitable, depending on your own situation.

Some readers will be members of groups who are also interested in working with the material, or at least some of the material, in this book. These may be church groups or occult lodges, and you may even have a study group specifically organized to work with this book. If that's the case, while you may not be able to organize a street parade with floats and circus performances, you can at least have a party, or two, or three.

If you don't have a group of that sort, you can spend this time celebrating with your family. Relax some of the rules, allow your children to stay up late, invite guests over for a barbecue—you don't even need to tell them the reason.

If you're on your own, you can still celebrate during this season. Again, no one has to know you're doing it—your coworkers don't need to know that you treated yourself to a night out or an extra dessert, or that you plan on doing so regularly between Septuagesima—a word they've likely never heard before—and Shrove Tuesday. The point is to allow yourself to both relax and enjoy this time and also to prepare for the spiritual disciplines of Lent.

Shrove Tuesday

The conclusion of Gesimatide is Shrove Tuesday, the last day before Ash Wednesday. You may know it by the name of Mardi Gras, this being one of those odd cases where the French name is better known than the English, at least in the United States. "Shrove Tuesday" is the traditional English name. The word "shrove" refers to the practice of being "shriven" of one's sins—in other words, of going to Confession. This was traditionally done today, as the first step in the Lenten purifications.

Practice for Shrove Tuesday

This day above all exemplified the dualistic nature of the pre-Lent season. Under the name of Mardi Gras, it is the name of a party, in fact one of the biggest and best-attended parties in the world. Meanwhile, the name of Shrove Tuesday refers to Sacramental Confession, which, as anyone who has received it can tell you, is about as far from a party as anyone can get!

In our own lives and practices, we can lean into both sides of the symbolism of this day.

Most of us don't live near New Orleans or any other city which has a large Mardi Gras celebration. If you do, don't be afraid to attend. If not—as is likely the case—you still have options, as you have had during the preceding few weeks. You can hold a party and invite your friends, or simply have a special dinner with your family. If you're going to be fasting from meat, this is a great opportunity to make a big meal, and invite enough guests to make sure there are no leftovers!

At the same time, today is also a day to attend Confession. If you either don't have access to a church which offers the sacrament of Confession or prefer not to participate, you can still get many of the benefits of Confession by practicing on your own.

At the beginning of this section, we presented the Confiteor Ritual. Today is the day to put this ritual into practice.

The following ritual is intended to accomplish as many of the effects of Confession as possible while working on your own. If at all possible, you should practice it today, on Shrove Tuesday, and be prepared to put it into practice once a week during Lent.

The confiteor ritual

Preparation. Make a List. Especially the first time you do this, it is best to focus on one particular sin or group of sins at a time. If it's been years, or decades, since you've considered your own failings, and you try to go through everything, you're going to be at this for a very long time. It can be very helpful to list your sins beforehand, so that you can focus on one or a few at a time.

As we are still in the pre-Lent season, your altar should be covered with a *green* cloth.

Step 1. Open a temple as you have been instructed.

Step 2. Relax your body, and use rhythmic breathing to enter into meditation.

Now, call to mind your sins. In some cases, these will be general patterns of bad behavior and mistakes. Every time you do this, expect a few specific things to come to mind. Things you've heard about times you were lazy or neglectful, drinking or playing video games when you should have been getting work done. In each of these cases, take a moment to imagine the situation from the perspective of the other people who were involved. Understand how your actions affected them, and how, even if they hurt you, they could not have done any different, given the circumstances. Forgive them, and ask God to forgive them. Many times, of course, you will be the one affected by your actions. Commit to forgiving yourself and asking God to forgive you.

Step 3. Say a Confiteor prayer. I've provided three examples, and encourage you to choose the one that best suits your needs and your practice. Each will work, but the symbolism is slightly different.

The Roman Catholic Confiteor:

> I confess to almighty God, to blessed Mary ever Virgin, [to blessed Saint Michael the Archangel, to blessed John the Baptist, to the holy Apostles Peter and Paul, and all the saints, that I have greatly sinned in thought, word, and deed: through my fault, through my fault, through my most grievous fault. (Strike your heart center three times while saying this.) Therefore I pray blessed Mary ever Virgin, blessed Michael the Archangel, blessed John the Baptist, the holy Apostles Peter and Paul, and all the saints, to pray for me to the Lord our God.

Note: During the part in brackets [ ], you may substitute other saints, such as those of your particular tradition or the patron saints of yourself, your family and your craft or trade.

The Anglican General Confession:

> Almighty and most merciful Father; we have erred, and strayed from thy ways like lost sheep. We have followed too much the devices and desires of my own heart. We have offended against thy holy laws. We have left undone those things which we ought to have done; And we have done those things which we ought not to have done; And there is no health in us. But thou, O Lord,

have mercy upon us, miserable offenders. Spare thou them, O God, which confess their faults. Restore thou them that are penitent; According to thy promises declared unto mankind in Christ Jesus our Lord. And grant, O most merciful Father, for his sake; That we may hereafter live a godly, righteous and sober life. To the Glory of thy holy Name. Amen

The Liberal Catholic Confiteor:

O Lord, Thou hast created us to be immortal and made us to be an image of Thine own eternity; yet often we forget the glory of our heritage and wander from the path which leads to righteousness. But Thou, O Lord, hast made us for Thyself and our hearts are ever restless till they find their rest in Thee. Look with the eyes of Thy love upon our manifold imperfections and pardon all our shortcomings, that we may be filled with the brightness of the everlasting light and become the unspotted mirror of Thy power and the image of Thy goodness; through Christ our Lord. Amen.

Step 4. Now, imagine a tiny light, like a candle flame, at the very center of your heart. This light is the grace of God within you, the healing mercy of Christ within you. Imagine it slowly expanding. It fills your heart, bringing warmth, healing, and blessing. It expands outward, filling your body, your head, your arms and your legs, healing and blessing every part of you. It expands, filling your aura, until you feel yourself surrounded by a sphere of holy fire. From there, it extends outward, bringing the healing mercy of God to every single person who has been harmed by your sins.

Do this slowly, and allow yourself to forgive others, to forgive yourself, and be forgiven by God. Know that God loves you in this moment, precisely as you are.

Step 5. For a time, take a moment and simply rest in the healing mercy of God. When you are ready, rise to your feet. Say the words:

May Almighty God have mercy on us, forgive us our sins, and lead us to everlasting life. Amen.

This concludes the ritual.

CHAPTER FOUR

Lent

In this section, we begin our Lenten practice. We will start by discussing the purpose of the Lenten Fast. We will look at Lent both from the mainstream or exoteric Christian perspective, but we will emphasize the alternative or esoteric tradition. Next, we will present instructions on the special practices associated with the Lenten season.

The next part contains the core of the work in this book, as we progress from Ash Wednesday to the vigil of Maundy Thursday. Each of the six Sundays of Lent is discussed in detail. Building on our earlier discussion, we will discuss the six Sundays as images of the six days of Creation, building up to the seventh, Easter, on which God completes his work by taking his throne. We will provide the Gospel readings for each Sunday, as well as the Introit to the Mass for that day. The Introit and Gospel are both taken from the Tridentine rite of the Mass, as this does not change from one year to the next and therefore allows us to continue and deepen our work year over year.

This section concludes with special practices for Maundy Thursday, Good Friday and Holy Saturday. Easter itself, which follows these, begins the next section of the book.

The Nature and purpose of Lent

The liturgical year begins with Advent, late in the year. This is a time of darkness and cold, when Nature herself seems to be dying. The cold deepens, the nights lengthen as we slide toward the Winter Solstice. And then, at Christmas, the light is reborn. On December 25, two days after the Solstice, the day is visibly longer than the night for the first time—though only just.

We continue through the long Christmas feast into ordinary time, pausing to celebrate the feasts of Candlemas, of Saints Brigid and Blaise. If we are fortunate enough to have been born in a Catholic country, we may experience a pleasant Carnival season in late February. All this time, in the Northern world, the days are lengthening, the snows are retreating—only to reveal a barren and empty world.

The desolation of early Spring is the reflection in nature of the Lenten Fast, which commemorates Christ's retreat into the desert following his baptism.

At Easter, finally, all things are renewed, and this time of renewal and rebirth is seen both in the visible world of nature and the invisible world of the spirit and the spiritual life. This is the unity of all things made possible by the Cross of Christ.

In the old tradition, every feast is preceded by a fast, every fast followed by a feast. This is the rhythm of life; as Spring follows Winter and Summer gives way to Autumn, so does the liturgical cycle precede from fast to feast, from feast to fast. The Lenten season is especially the season of penance, and before we go any further, we ought to talk about what that means.

The Lenten Fast

The 40 days of the Lenten Fast commemorate the 40 days that Christ spent fasting in the wilderness, following his baptism. Discussing the Lenten Fast in his monumental work *The Liturgical Year*, the French Benedictine Dom Prosper Gueranger wrote:

> Thus does our Saviour go before us on the holy path of Lent. He has borne all its fatigues and hardships, that so we, when called upon to tread the narrow way of our Lenten Penance, might have His example wherewith to silence the excuses, and sophisms,

and repugnances, of self-love and pride. The lesson is here too plainly given not to be understood; the law of doing penance for sin is here too clearly shown, and we cannot plead ignorance; let us honestly accept the teaching and practise it. Jesus leaves the Desert where he had spent the Forty Days, and begins his preaching with these words, which he addresses to all men: Do penance, for the Kingdom of heaven is at hand [St. Matthew iv. 17]. Let us not harden our hearts to this invitation, lest there be fulfilled in us the terrible threat contained in those other words of our Redeemer: Unless ye shall do penance, ye shall perish [St. Luke, xiii. 3].

Now, in the verse in Luke's Gospel referenced, "do penance" is *metanoēte*. This refers back to the concept *metanoia*, "the changing of the *nous*." The *nous* is the highest part of the soul, the part that extends upward into the realm above the soul, the habitation of the angels and saints of God. Some of the ancient writers refer to nous as "the eye of the soul," because it perceives the spiritual reality. In our current condition, our nous is clouded, and we see perceive the spiritual reality "through a glass, darkly." Most of the time our attention is fixed on the things of the visible world, which we perceive with our physical eyes and which is a mere shadow of the True Reality of Spirit. Lent is a season for *metanoia*, changing the condition of our nous, clearing away the detritus of sin which clouds it, and re-directing our attention toward the spiritual world.

Lent and the Law of Rhythm

Here is a little bit of occult philosophy, from an early 20th-century text called *The Kybalion*:

> The pendulum of the clock swings a certain distance to the right, and then an equal distance to the left. The seasons balance each other in the same way. The tides follow the same Law. And the same Law is manifested in all the phenomena of Rhythm. The pendulum, with a short swing in one direction, has but a short swing in the other; while the long swing to the right invariably means the long swing to the left. An object hurled upward to a certain height has an equal distance to traverse on its return. The force with which a projectile is sent upward a mile is reproduced when the projectile

> returns to the earth on its return journey. This Law is constant on the Physical Plane, as reference to the standard authorities will show you.
>
> But the Hermetists carry it still further. They teach that a man's mental states are subject to the same Law.

Easter is the greatest feast of the Christian church. To say that is not to say that it's a great party—it's far more than a good time. During the Easter Triduum, we enter into and participate in the crucifixion, death, and Resurrection of Our Lord. To truly enter into the Mystery of Easter is to exalt our spirits far beyond any pleasure of the flesh or any wonder of the astral or psychic worlds.

The Kybalion continues:

> [The ancient masters] teach that before one is able to enjoy a certain degree of pleasure, he must have swung as far, proportionately, toward the other pole of feeling. They hold, however, that the Negative is precedent to the Positive in this matter, that is to say that in experiencing a certain degree of pleasure it does not follow that he will have to "pay up for it" with a corresponding degree of pain; on the contrary, the pleasure is the Rhythmic swing, according to the Law of Compensation, for a degree of pain previously experienced either in the present life, or in a previous incarnation.

If we put this idea into practice, the difficulties and austerities of Lent become a kind of slingshot, intended to launch us upward as far as we can go at Easter. It follows that the more we enter into the penitential side of Lent, the more effectively we will be "launched upward" at Eastertime.

Again, remember that it isn't just any pain we seek, or any pleasure; this isn't sadomasochism. We aren't looking simply to hurt ourselves any more than we are simply hoping to have a good time at Easter. It is spiritual, and not physical "pleasure" that we seek. Moreover, we must be very careful not to limit our works of fasting during Lent to the material body, because if we do, this will lead directly to sin. How? Because the slingshot will propel us from pain to pleasure, and if all we've done is to give up a destructive pleasure, we will find ourselves mired in it all the worse come Easter! In order to have lasting results, the focus of our work must be spiritual, and not material—or at least, not *merely* material.

Lent and the training of the will

Through the Lenten Fast, we also train and fortify our will. Now, the will gets a bad rap among some modern Christians. Rightly noting our Lord's words, "Thy Will, not mine be done," they therefore conclude that we ought not to have a will of our own. But this is based on a misunderstanding of our will and its nature.

Our very existence is provided for us by God, "in whom we live and move and have our being." To exist at all is to exist on account of God. Now, one of the characteristics of God in traditional Catholic as well as esoteric theology is *divine simplicity*. This means simply that God does not have parts. Everything we experience as a "part" of God is actually the whole of God. God's will, then, is not a separate substance, like an arm or a leg or even like a ray of light from a star. God's will is identical with his being. As God is the source of our being, our own True Will is also identical with the core of our being.

Now, from this, it is apparent that our will is not the same thing as our passions or our desires, as many think. In fact, it's very often exactly the opposite! Just as our being is derived from God's being, our True Will is derived from God's will and is God's will. So there isn't a contradiction between our will and God's will—When we say to God, "thy will, not mine be done," we mean "May I be as you intend me to be, which is what I truly am."

Lenten practice

Lenten practice is not limited to fasting. Rather, like Advent, Lent focuses on the three practices of fasting, prayer, and almsgiving. Lent also has a special emphasis on *repentance* and the purification of sin. As we discussed in the introduction to this book, this work of repentance and purification is rooted in the ancient Mystery traditions and is, indeed, the culmination of them. We will discuss each of these practices one at a time, beginning with fasting, and provide guides to each.

Before Lent itself begins, there is the short season of Gesimatide, which lasts a little over two weeks. This is a time of preparation, when we make ourselves ready for the season to come. We will discuss the Gesima season in the next chapter, but I want to present this material first, so that you can use Gesimatide to prepare for the Lenten season. Read through this material now, and then use the weeks from Septuagesima to Shrove Tuesday to decide on a plan for practice during Lent itself.

Lenten practice 1: Fasting

The best-known of all Lenten practices is the Lenten Fast. Though greatly degraded in modern times, this is still kept in a certain sense by the Church, and is kept in its full sense in the Eastern Orthodox tradition and by many traditional Catholics. Fasting is always a part of Lent. It is a necessary practice, and one we will follow in this book.

With that said, fasting can take many different forms. In this chapter, we're going to talk about how to fast and present a series of different fasting options. You will need to choose one, but it is important to select the one that is right for you. Pray to the Holy Spirit for guidance, and choose appropriately: There are no points for picking something which is either too difficult to sustain or which is unsuitable for your station in life.

We're going to use the general term "fasting" in this book, but you should know that it actually has two elements, called fasting and abstinence. Technically speaking, fasting means reducing the amount of food taken in a given time period, while abstinence means avoiding certain types of foods. The traditional Lenten Fast includes both fasting and abstinence, as we shall see. Before we commit to fasting, we should understand why we are doing it and what its purpose and effects are.

The traditional fast focuses, above all, on abstinence from *meat*, as well as a reduction in food intake. This has three major effects.

The first is, quite simply, a withdrawal from the Physical Plane. The human body is, of course, made of meat, though we don't often think of it this way. An old science fiction story pictures aliens whose bodies are composed of crystals or gas (it's not made clear in the text) arriving at Earth and reacting in horror: "They're made of meat." "Meat? How is that possible?" The aliens soon decide that Earth is better avoided.

In our tradition, we don't take quite this extreme an approach to our bodily condition. It is, nevertheless, the case that the human body is made of meat, and consuming meat has a "grounding" effect on the consciousness. That is to say, it makes us more aware of our body, and more aware of bodies in general.

From both a mainstream and an Esoteric Christian perspective, this is the way things are supposed to be. Angels are disembodied spirits: They can affect the Physical Plane, but the center of their consciousness is in the higher planes. The Human Being is different. Our consciousness is meant to extend from the heights of the spiritual plane, through the planes of dense matter. Now, both Esoteric and mainstream Christians agree that something has gone wrong with the plan. We are supposed to be embodied on the Physical Plane. The trouble is that we are effectively stuck here. It isn't that our bodies or the world are necessarily evil. Rather, it is like we are under house arrest. You may love your home, and you should, but you might like to go outside every now and then!

Abstaining from animal foods allows our consciousness to withdraw from physical embodiment and grants easier access to the higher planes of being.

Historically, the Christian fast also involved abstinence from alcohol. This was either never the case in the West, or it was abandoned at an early period. In any event, by the High Middle Ages we had something of the opposite in effect: Some of the very strong beers produced by monks in places like Belgium were actually designed as aids to fasting. By doubling or even quadrupling the amount of malted barley used in beer production, the monks produced a kind of liquid bread.

It is worth noting that, until the modern period, beers in the Western world were also frequently brewed using psychoactive herbs such as wild rosemary and mandrake root. It was only in modern times that beer production became standardized so that, under the German Beer Laws, only hops were allowed to be used as an adjunct—hops, whose primary effect is to produce drowsiness. Prior to this period, the use of alcoholic drinks during Lent probably had quite a different significance, especially for the work of withdrawing from the Physical Plane! As it stands now, whatever virtues alcoholic beverages had in the past are largely gone, and their deleterious effects remain. These destructive effects were well known in earlier times: In the ancient world, for example, when divination by reading dreams was more common, diviners knew to ignore the dreams of those who had consumed wine before bed. Abstaining from alcohol during Lent is not required but remains a good option for many people.

To return to our subject, the second purpose of fasting is simply to produce discipline.

To speak of "discipline" is often to conjure up images of stern-faced nuns, high school principals or even prison guards, enforcing an arbitrary authority. We should abandon this image. Discipline is essential in the spiritual life and has a specific spiritual meaning.

To understand this, we will need a bit of psychic anatomy: that is, literally, the structure of the soul.

An ancient understanding of the structure of the soul, detailed by the Greek philosopher Plato in his work *The Republic* divides the soul into three parts. These are called the *nous*, the *thymos*, and the *epithymia*. The nous is the center of thought, reason, and spiritual vision. It is centered at the head of man. The *thymos* is the center of the will, the vital spirits, and the social emotions. It is centered at the heart. And the third part, the *epithymia*, is the center of the bodily appetites, both for food and for sex; appropriately, it is located in the abdomen.

In a well-ordered soul, the nous rules with the aid of the *thymos*, like a wise monarch governing their domain with the aid of the warrior class. The *epithymia* is taken care of but not allowed to run riot, like a well-governed peasantry or working class.

Disorder in the soul is like anarchy in the kingdom. The will cooperates with the appetites, and the reason is shut away and silenced. It is like a kingdom in which the warrior class cooperates with the workers to cut off the head of the king, and everyone does what they please without regard for the consequences. The results, like the aftermath of a revolution, are anarchy, chaos, starvation and civil war.

Again, it is not that our appetites are necessarily bad or evil. Our natural desires for food and water, sex and sleep allow us to survive and propagate the species. It is, however, the case that our appetites must not control our actions. A bit of self-examination will prove this to be true. If you simply followed what you wanted to do from one moment to the next, what would your life look like? If you're anything at all like me, at the very best, you'd have four donuts for breakfast and spend your days "zoning out" in front of the television, with occasional breaks for beer and nicotine, ignoring the dishes, the laundry and the bills that slowly piled up around you. And, again, that's the very best possible result. Let's not speak of anything worse.

And so Lent allows us to *practice* disciplining our appetites. We shouldn't live this way all the time. In ordinary times, we should allow ourselves the pleasures that this life offers us. But, like a runner preparing for a marathon or a boxer training for a big fight, we will be successful in our spiritual life if we allow ourselves to take some time for serious training.

The third purpose of the Lenten Fast is perhaps more important than the other two. This is simply *to participate in the life of Christ*. Note that Lent is 40 days: This is the length of time during which, we are told, Our Lord fasted in the wilderness following his baptism by John. The purpose of the entire Christian tradition, as a Mystery religion, is the participation in the life of Christ, that we may share in His glory to the degree possible for us. We fast in order that we may imitate Him, as a part of that participation.

Finally, it's important to note that Lent as a whole is a time of *purification*. This is one of the most important elements of the cycle of the Mysteries. Before the initiation can be received, the initiate must be purified, which is achieved by fasting, Confession, and otherwise withdrawing from ordinary life. This was the case in all of the ancient Mystery cults, which prefigure Christianity, and it is just that much the more the case in the Christian tradition, the culmination of all the ancient Mysteries.

Now that we understand the purpose of our Lenten Fast, let's talk about what it might look like.

Fasting option 1: The traditional fast

The traditional fast has two parts, as we discussed above: Fasting and Abstinence.

As we saw above, the *fasting* part of the Fast involves limiting the amount of food taken every day. The usual prescription is as follows:

- One small meal, totaling no more than 8 ounces.
- Two light snacks.
- A morning cup of tea or coffee with toast is also permitted.

The *abstinence* portion of the traditional fast is limited to avoiding meat. Fish, eggs, and dairy products generally may be taken. The main meal, then, may consist of a four-ounce fillet of salmon with rice and vegetables on the side. That's not so bad, all things considered.

Note that the traditional fast doesn't require abstinence from alcohol. Again, as described above, alcoholic beverages may be taken. In recent years, some people have accomplished the traditional fast by living entirely on stout beer such as Guinness. I don't recommend this, but it's worth noting.

Fasting option 2: The traditional fast, Orthodox version

In the Christian East, a more severe version of the fast has been maintained. In addition to abstaining from meat, the Orthodox also avoid all fish and dairy products, maintaining a vegan diet. They also avoid alcohol of any kind, and even cooking oil!

If you are tempted to try this form of fasting, please note that it is very difficult and can have serious negative consequences for your health. In the Orthodox world, neither laity nor clergy are allowed to undertake the fast without guidance from a spiritual director. Many Orthodox priests have stories about severe rebukes they received when attempting the fast without permission and guidance; some have even been barred from fasting for doing so.

Fasting option 3: Screen fasting

In earlier times, the great spiritual need was one of withdrawal from the natural world to the supernatural world, which is above and prior to Nature. Our own time is a bit different. Many of us spend our entire lives in temperature-controlled rooms, insulated from the world outside, and spend many hours a day focused on screens: computer screens, televisions, smart phones.

Our change in circumstances is such that even our appetites have become aligned with this artificial world, so that now we crave the cheap satisfactions of Instagram or TikTok, social media, or a Netflix binge even more than we crave food or drink or sex. It is important to note how severe this situation is. Artificial things are different from natural things.

To understand this, consider the difference between a tree and a house.

Left to its own devices, a tree will eventually fall over and decompose into soil. It can also be cut down to build a house. Either way, the tree is dead. But here is the difference: If the tree falls over on its own, it will eventually produce a new tree, as its seeds sprout or some element of life in its roots sends forth a new sapling. But when a house falls over, it never produces a new house. At best, if some seed of the tree that was cut down to build it remains lodged in its wood, it may produce a new tree!

From our perspective, this means that the *tree* has something in it which the house does not. This *something* is what we call Nature. It is the principle of life, marked by stability—the tree remains a tree, even if its branches fall—and change—it both grows and reproduces itself. The house does not have this principle in it. Our modern technologies are even worse than this. The house is what it seems to be: A place in which people live. Technological devices like cell phones and computers are different. Their purpose is not even that which they appear to be. We don't use them as mirrors or paperweights. Instead, we use them to access an artificial world whose existence is far more ephemeral and unreal than earlier artificial things like houses or even cars.

And the nature of these technologies is such that we who use them are constantly craving them, very often acting like drug addicts in search of our next "fix."

In this situation, it could be argued that fasting from technology has become even more important than fasting from food or from alcohol. I therefore strongly recommend fasting from technology, which I simply call screenfasting, whether or not you participate in the more traditional forms of fasting.

Now, what this looks like in practice is going to depend on your own circumstances, including your job and your relationship to modern technology. In my own life, for example, I find internet politics very addictive. I crave information on the latest news and the latest quarrels that define our political life. When I get out of control, I find myself browsing Twitter and political websites for hours, sometimes barely comprehending what I'm reading—and focusing more on the bad news than on the good. I therefore make it a point during fasting seasons to completely avoid any websites which could possibly include any news or political speculations.

You might be different. You might be addicted to internet shopping. You might spend a lot of time looking at online pornography. Or you might just be sick of wasting time watching Netflix or responding to text messages. You will, therefore, need to come up with a different way of fasting from screens, suitable for your own life and your own needs.

Fasting option 4: The modern fast

The modern Catholic Church does not really prescribe fasting during Lent, except on the days of Ash Wednesday and Good Friday. Instead, it prescribes two things: The first is abstaining from meat on Fridays during Lent, and the second is giving up ... something. Yes, it's that general: You could give up anything from chocolate to swearing in order to fit the fasting requirements.

I'm being a bit flippant, but the truth is that even this form of fasting can have very beneficial effects on the soul. I know someone who committed to not saying or thinking anything negative about other people for the duration of Lent. In a certain sense, this is against the traditional spirit of Lent, because eating meat is a good thing which is given up for the sake of a higher good, while saying unkind things about other people is a bad thing. Nevertheless, the cause of a thing is known by its effect, and I can tell you that this practice had a very good effect on the soul of the person who undertook it. We can therefore know that the effect being goodness, the cause was also good. If the modern fast is what you can do, then it is what you should do. If you undertake it sincerely and with dedication, it will have better results than a different fast undertaken half-heartedly.

Before Ash Wednesday, pick one of the fasting options given above, and commit to sticking with it throughout the whole of Lent.

Lenten practice 2: Almsgiving

The benefits of fasting are numerous. In the struggle to maintain our fast, we learn discipline; in learning to do without things that we are used to, we discover our strength. If all we're doing is fasting, however, then what we're doing is no different from dieting or reading a self-help book.

Don't knock those sorts of things. A person who becomes better from laying off the sugar or reading *The Seven Habits of Highly Effective People* makes the whole world a little bit better. These practices, however, have their limits. At their very best, they can produce a person who is happier, more successful, and much easier for other people to get along with. At their worst, however, they can produce a high-functioning narcissist.

And so in addition to fasting, Lenten practice requires *almsgiving*.

As in the case of fasting, this has certain effects. It also needs to be approached carefully and mindfully.

In general, there are two forms of giving: giving money or goods, and giving time or service. Since every good costs money and all services require time, we'll simplify things by saying that we can give money or time or both.

Tell me if this sounds familiar: When you hear about "almsgiving," the first thing you think of is either donating money to a nonprofit or volunteering at a soup kitchen. Those are definitely the first things that I think of. But giving is *not* limited to these things. Many people don't have the money to make a serious donation to a charitable organization.

Many times, a small donation could do more good *not* given to a large charity.

The same can be said of donations of *time*. Some of us have time to work at a soup kitchen or food pantry, but this isn't the only way that we can donate our time.

Imagine that you had 50 dollars to give. You could donate it to a large charity which does good work. That's a great thing to do, and if you feel called to, you should do it. On the other hand, what if you gave the same 50 dollars as a tip to a waitress or barista? If you've ever worked in the food service industry, you know how hard it can be, how rude customers can be, and how much people in that industry struggle to make ends meet. You also know what a difference a substantial tip could make—especially during a holiday season.

Again, time is the same. It may be that you could do great work by volunteering at a food pantry or a homeless shelter. It may also be the case, however, that there is a park or woodland near your home which is littered with trash that no one has cleaned up. Or it may be the case that you know a lonely, elderly, or just a difficult person who has no one to talk to. In cases like those, donating your time can make a real, noticeable difference. You can clean up a park, by the way, without asking anyone's permission, organizing a group, or posting a sign on the freeway. You can just show up one day with gloves and a trash bag. And you can call your lonely grandmother or estranged friend any time—even right now, if you want. These are donations of time which can make an enormous difference in people's lives. Best of all, it's easier to do these sorts of donations *anonymously*. If you volunteer at a food pantry, people are likely to find out about it. If you simply call a friend on the phone, you don't have to say anything about the reason you called: "I just wanted to see how you're doing." Remember: "When you give alms, do not let your left hand know what your right hand is doing, so that your alms may be in secret; and your Father who sees in secret will reward you."

Practice

Make a donation of time or money at least once a week during Lent. Thursdays are a good day for this, if you need a day to help you stick to the routine. If you miss a week, don't fret: Just make two donations the following week.

Lenten practice 3: Repentance

The three basic Christian spiritual practices are prayer, fasting, and almsgiving. We have already discussed prayer. If you haven't established a prayer rule, now is the time. In addition to ordinary daily prayer, however, during Lent, we specifically emphasize the work of *repentance*.

As in the case of discipline, this is a big topic, often misunderstood, and so we're going to have to discuss what repentance really means and how we can do it.

The Nature of repentance

Let's start by defining our terms. We first meet the word "Repentance" in the Gospels in the beginning of Matthew:

In those days came John the Baptist, saying, "Repent, for the kingdom of Heaven is at hand."

In the English-speaking world, the words "repent" and "repentance" very often are pictured as meaning "Say you're sorry." "The kingdom of Heaven is at hand," meanwhile, tells us why we should say that we're sorry: Because God's about to turn up and you're going to get your butt kicked.

Needless to say, this isn't a very helpful way of understanding things, most of the time.

Now, the word used in Greek and translated into English as "repent" is *metanoia*. The literal meaning is "change your *nous*." This is sometimes rendered, "change your heart" in English, and that gets at the sense of it better than the word "repent."

We repent by changing our hearts. Literally, by changing our *nous*, the part of our soul that both reasons and can directly experience the Divine. And why must we do this? Because "the kingdom of Heaven is at hand." In other words, because God and the Communion of His Saints are among us, around us, within us. If we change the orientation of our psyches, they will be present to us.

There are a few means by which we can do this, and this is where the tradition is actually very helpful. The practice of confessing one's sins is often pictured as simply a way of "Saying you're sorry" and accepting your punishment. There is much more to it than that. Sin, as we will see, consists of patterns of behavior which draw us away from God and toward the Chaos that is the bottom of reality, next to nonexistence. By Confession, we accomplish a number of things. First, we identify the patterns of behavior which are keeping us from awareness of God and the spiritual reality around us. Second, we act to heal the damage that sin causes to our souls and the souls of others who are affected by our sins. Third, we restore the relationships which exist on a subtle, spiritual level between ourselves and others. Finally, we invoke the healing power of God into our souls to restore us to a semblance of our original condition.

Now, how should we accomplish this repentance?

One option is simply to go and receive Sacramental Confession from a priest. The Catholic Church makes this sacrament available, though sometimes hard to find, to its parishioners. The Anglican churches also offer the sacrament of Confession. This is a great option if it's available to you. It may not be. In that case, we will need to do some work on our own.

The second option is one which you have already encountered. This is the *Confiteor Ritual*, which we began to work with on Shrove Tuesday. Both this ritual and the Forgiveness Ritual can be practiced throughout Lent.

Practice

The Confiteor Ritual should be practiced once per week during Lent. Saturday is a good day to do this, but any day will do. If you miss a week, don't fret, just make sure you go or perform the ritual next week. The Forgiveness Ritual can be performed again any time you feel the need for it. Both of these rituals work to heal our relationships, both with God and our fellow human beings.

Lenten practice 4: Lenten devotion: Via Dolorosa

Via Dolorosa or the Way of the Cross, often simply called the Stations of the Cross in English, is a traditional Catholic devotional and one of the few that remains well preserved in the modern American Church. It consists of 14 separate stations, each of which contains an image from the last hours of Jesus's earthly life. The Stations begin with Jesus being condemned to death by Pilate and the Sanhedrin, and end with his death at Calvary. At each station, certain prayers are said.

During Lent, it's very common for churches to pray the Stations of the Cross publicly. Many larger shrines also have large outdoor Stations of the Cross, which can be walked individually.

The Stations make an excellent devotion during Lent, and you can practice them as often as you like, or at least every Friday. You may not be able to get to a church or shrine with the stations, but you can pray the stations privately, in your magical temple or in your home.

The Stations of the Cross

First Station. Jesus is condemned to death by Pontius Pilate.

Second Station. Jesus takes up his cross and begins his journey to Golgotha.

Third Station. Jesus Falls the First Time.

Fourth Station. Jesus Meets with His Sorrowful Mother.

Fifth Station. Saint Simon of Cyrene Helps Jesus Carry the Cross.

Sixth Station. Saint Veronica Wipes the Face of Jesus.

Seventh Station. Jesus Falls the Second Time.

Eighth Station. Jesus Comforts the Women of Jerusalem.

Ninth Station. Jesus Falls the Third Time.

Tenth Station. Jesus Is Stripped of His Garments.

Eleventh Station. Jesus Is Nailed to the Cross.

Twelfth Station. Jesus Dies on the Cross.

Thirteenth Station. Jesus Is Taken Down from the Cross.

Fourteenth Station. Jesus Is Laid in the Tomb.

The way of the Cross meditation

Preparation. This meditation is fairly flexible. It can be performed in an open magical temple, with incense burning and candles lit, or you can simply begin with the Banishing Sign of the Cross and continue into the meditation while seated on your living room couch. You can also practice the Way of the Cross meditation without any special preparation, or even in a public place, like a park bench or a city bus. Many Catholic supply companies sell holy cards with the images of the 14 stations printed on them, and you can also find images of the Stations online, which you can print out for your use at home. If you don't have a set of images, however, you can simply use the description in this chapter.

If you are working with a temple, remember that the color for the altar cloth throughout Lent is *violet*.

Step 1. Make the Sign of the Cross, and say the Our Father, three Hail Marys, and the Glory Be.

Step 2. If you are practicing in an open temple, stand, and raise your hands in the orans posture. Say the words:

> We adore thee Oh Christ, and we praise thee, for by thy cross thou hast redeemed the world. May I walk alongside thee on the Way of the Cross, and may the Holy Spirit guide my meditations. Amen.

Step 3. Announce the name of the first station, "Jesus is condemned to death by Pontius Pilate." You can say this out loud or silently, as it suits your needs and the context. If you're working in a temple or in a private place, you will want to say the words out loud; if you're in a public park or on a city bus, it is probably best to simply say it silently to yourself.

Step 4. Take a moment to still your thoughts, and then visualize the scene described: In this case, imagine the scene as Pilate, despite his reluctance, hands Jesus over to the chief priests to be crucified.

Step 5. Say the Our Father, Hail Mary, and Glory Be.

Step 6. Repeat steps 3, 4, and 5 for all of the remaining stations.

Step 7. After you complete the 14th station, take a moment to pause and reflect on the whole of the Way of the Cross. Then say the following prayer:

> By thy passion and cross, Oh Lord, thou hast redeemed the world.
> May I walk with thee on the Way of the Cross,
> This day and every day,
> Dying to the world of Sin and Death,
> May I be born into the life of the Spirit. Amen.

Step 8. Close with the Sign of the Cross. If you are working in an open temple, close it in the usual way.

Ash Wednesday

Memento, homo, quia pulvis es, et in pulveram reverteris.

Remember, O Man, that thou art dust, and to dust thou shalt return.

These are the words spoken (traditionally) by the priest as he traces a cross of ashes on the forehead of each parishioner on Ash Wednesday. The ashes themselves are made from the palms of the previous year's Palm Sunday, burned to ash in a sacred fire, and consecrated with special blessings.

Ashes are an ancient sign of repentance, found in a number of places in the Old Testament (Jonah 3:5–9, Jeremiah 6:26). Historically, the use of ashes was accompanied by the wearing of a coarse, uncomfortable fabric called sackcloth. This is the origin of the phrase "sackcloth and ashes," which remains in our language, though, fortunately, wearing sackcloth itself is no longer required.

The meaning of Ashes

In the ritual of Ash Wednesday, consecrated ashes are placed in the form of a cross on the forehead of the initiate. This particular point is significant, as it relates to the third eye. The third eye was known in the Western world as well as in the East. The part of the soul called the *nous* is known as the "eye of the soul," and its nature is to perceive spiritual reality. In traditional psychic anatomy, the nous is located in the head, corresponding to the third eye. There is, moreover, evidence that the term "third eye" itself was used in the West as well as the East. The early Christian writer Origen, in his *Cóntra Celsum*, tells us that Plato used the term, and the Platonic tradition in philosophy was concerned with the *nous* and the higher levels of reality of which it perceives.

The placement of the ashes at this point, then, at once symbolizes penitence, helps to activate the psychic faculties. This is done at the beginning of Lent, and is followed by a sustained withdrawal from the ordinary concerns of the material world. Traditionally, and for many today, this also includes abstinence from meat, which roots the soul in the material body. This withdrawal from the material is then accompanied by works of repentance (metanoia), which unite the inner faculties of the soul with the Eternal Will of God. To atone for sin means to gather the dis-united parts of the self and bring the whole soul under the command of the nous, itself aware of and united to the Will of God.

The initiate, addressed as homo, "human," is reminded that he is dust. What is dust? The human, and everything pertaining to it. The body and the possessions. But also the desires, the habits, the preferences, the thoughts—all are dust. Only the Divine is immortal, and only that within us which participates in the divine can be immortal. Everything else is dust and ashes. The old human was Adam, who died and descended into the Earth, which is to say, into the material body. The new human is Christ, who will die and rise again, overcoming death by death. We have all been Adam and Eve. In the Mysteries of Christmas, we become Mary, and bring forth the Christ-Child. Now we must become Christ, and follow Him on the road to Calvary. It is not an easy road, but at the end of it is the Resurrection and Life Eternal.

The ashes, placed on the forehead, are made from the burned fronds of last year's palms. The palms, we recall, were laid at the feet of Christ, and will be laid at the feet of Christ, as he enters into Jerusalem. Alive then, they are now ashes, and this year there will be new palms, and next year, new ashes. Thus, the cycle continues. As the palms are burned year after year, so many will strive this year, which is to say, this lifetime, and fall short. They will burn, and then they will try again, and again, and again, unto the end of the age. Until all are saved from the fire.

Ash Wednesday in esoteric Christianity

As we saw at Christmas, Adam and Eve are, in a sense, a single person, Adam–Eve. Adam represents the higher part of the soul, the *nous*; Eve, born from his chest, represents the middle and lower parts of the soul. Turning toward material creation in obedience to Desire, the Serpent, the Human Adam–Eve sins. Turning away from the Eternal, the Human Being is trapped in matter, doomed to struggle perpetually with Desire, to die and return to dust, and return to life again.

Repenting, purifying, turning again toward Eternal things over the long course of the Earthly sojourn, the Human Being is born now as Mary. Once again, the Human Being is sinless (Immaculate) and unencumbered by desire (Virgin). As Adam brought forth Eve from his chest, so Mary brings forth Christ from her womb, signifying that the soul is now purified unto its lowest parts, and now turns only toward eternal things. Before, the *nous* was masculine, which is to say, active; now the nous becomes feminine, receptive to the Will of God. The Desire, signified in the body by the lower dantien, is altogether purified and turned toward the higher.

Now, at the beginning of Lent, the adult Christ is the New Adam, the restored humanity, beginning the process by which the chains of matter will be overcome, and mankind restored to the Eternal.

It is a good practice to attend Mass or services on Ash Wednesday. At Catholic churches, ashes are offered freely, even where Communion is not. Anglican churches are even more open, and those in the Anglo-Catholic tradition also offer a liturgy in English which is both more beautiful and more magically effective than that of most of their Roman counterparts.

As always, however, you may either be unable to attend a public service or prefer to practice on your own. If that's the case, you may make use of the following ritual.

The ritual of Ashes

Preparation. The preparation for this ritual is a little more involved than some, as you will need ashes to work with. If you have a blessed palm (or branches from another tree) from last year's Palm Sunday, you can make use of this.

In order to reduce Palm Sunday branches to ashes, you will need some equipment and space in which to work. Specifically, you'll need a cast-iron pan and an open fire as a heat source. A gas or charcoal grill works well, as does a backyard fire pit or a campfire, provided you have a metal grill which can be placed over the fire itself. Make sure that the pan is either new or thoroughly cleaned with soap. It will help if you douse the plant material in strong alcohol of 150 proof or greater.

Start by performing the Banishing Sign of the Cross. Then place the plant material in the cast-iron pan, say the asperges prayer, and sprinkle the plant material three times with holy water. Apply the alcohol, and set the pan over the fire. Be careful; the material will catch fire quickly. For best results, use a clean metal stir (metal rods sold as skewers for meat work well) and stir the material while it turns to ash.

Warning: The process of burning plant material like this is called *calcining*, and is a part of the work of plant alchemy. Calcining plants or herbs produces an enormous amount of smoke and should *never* be done indoors.

If you either do not have Palm Sunday branches available or if the process of reducing them to ash is beyond your capabilities at this time, you can use incense ash. In this case, follow the steps above, performing the Banishing Sign of the Cross and sprinkling the incense with holy water. Then simply light it and let it burn down, collecting the ashes when you are done.

Once you have your ashes ready, either from palm fronds or from incense, you will need to bless them, using the following ritual.

The blessing of Ashes

Preparation. Set up a working space for a magical temple, with your ashes placed in a glass or ceramic container on the altar. The altar cloth should be violet, even if you are performing this ritual the day before Ash Wednesday.

Step 1. Open your temple as instructed above.

Step 2. With hands raised in the orans posture, say the following words:

> In Him was Life, and the Life was the Light of Men.
> Almighty Father, the light of thy truth shines in the darkness, and bestows sight to the eyes of the sinner. Grant us the gift of thy light this day and the mercy of thy forgiveness, as we enter into this season of repentance.

Step 2. Turn your attention to the ashes, and hold your hands over them. Say the following words. When you come to a + make the Sign of the Cross over the ashes with your right hand, visualizing the cross in brilliant white light.

> Almighty and everlasting God, we beseech thee to spare them that are penitent, and to be favorable to them that call upon thee. Vouchsafe, we pray thee, to send thy holy Angel from heaven to bless + and sanctify + these ashes, that they may be a wholesome medicine to all them that humbly call upon thy holy Name, who in their consciences by sin are accused, who in the sight of thy heavenly mercy bewail their sins, and earnestly and meekly implore thy gracious loving kindness. And we beseech thee to grant to all them that call upon thy holy Name, that being sprinkled with these ashes for the remission of their sins, they may be preserved evermore both in body and soul. Through Jesus Christ our Lord, Amen.

Step 3. Sprinkle the ashes three times with holy water, and cense them three times with incense. (To do this, you can either pick up the vessel containing the ashes and pass it through times the incense smoke.)

The ashes are now ready for use. You may *either* close your temple, if you've prepared the ashes in advance, *or* proceed to the next section.

The ritual of Ash Wednesday

Preparation. Set up your temple as instructed, making sure that you have blessed ashes on the altar.

Step 1. Open a temple as instructed, unless you are proceeding directly from the Blessing of Ashes.

Step 2. Stand, raise your hands in the *orans* posture, and say the following words:

> As we enter into the season of Lent I pray, Oh Lord, that I may begin the work of fasting and repentance with true piety and persevere to the end with steadfast devotion. Through Christ, our Lord. Amen.

Step 3. Read the day's Gospel, out loud or silently, which is from Matthew, 6:16–21:

> At that time, Jesus said to His disciples: When you fast, be not as the hypocrites, sad. For they disfigure their faces, that they may appear unto men to fast. Amen, I say to you, they have received their reward. But thou, when thou fastest, anoint thy head and wash thy face, that thou appear not to men to fast, but to thy Father who is in secret: and thy Father who seeth in secret will repay thee. Lay not up to yourselves treasures on Earth: where the rust and moth consume, and where thieves break through and steal. But lay up to yourselves treasures in Heaven: where neither the rust nor the moth doth consume, and where the thieves do not break through nor steal. For where thy treasure is, there is thy heart also.

Step 4. Take a moment to pause and gather your energies. Then, dip your thumb in the ashes and draw a cross, in ashes, on your forehead. Say the words:

> *Memorem qui pulvis sum, et in pulverim revertero.*
>
> May I remember that I am dust, and to dust I shall return.

Step 5. Sit down and enter into meditation. Consider the ashes and their symbolism, as described above; the Gospel; and anything else that comes to mind about the season of Lent and the symbolism of Ash Wednesday.

Step 6. When you are ready, come out of meditation. Stand, and offer the following prayer:

> He that shall meditate day and night upon the Law of the Lord, shall bring forth his fruit in due season. May the Holy Spirit guide me in my meditations in this Lenten season, and may I die to the Lower Self and bring forth the fruit of the Higher Life at Easter.

Step 7. Close your temple in the usual way.

During the days between now and the First Sunday of Lent, continue to consider the themes of Ash Wednesday in your daily meditations.

The First Sunday of Lent

The First Sunday of Lent is known as Brand Sunday, or, alternatively, as Invocabit Sunday. The term Brand Sunday comes from the Middle Ages, when young people who had taken the Carnival celebrations to excess were expected to appear at the church on this Sunday with a burning torch or "brand." The term Invocabit comes from the Introit to the Mass, which reads as follows:

> *Invocabit me, et ego exaudiam eum: eripiam eum et glorificabo eum: longitudine dierum adimplebo eum.*
>
> He shall cry unto me, and I shall hear him: I will deliver him, and I will glorify him: I will fill him with length of days.

The First Sunday of Lent is a most solemn occasion, the true beginning of our Lenten journey. Remember that we are re-creating the world. On Ash Wednesday, we have returned to ashes, which is to say, to the Chaos prior to creation. This Sunday is the first day, the day on which God said, Let there be light.

> And God saw the light, that it was good: and God divided the light from the darkness. And God called the light Day, and the darkness he called Night. And the evening and the morning were the first day.

Our work this week is to separate the darkness from the light in our own lives. During the pre-Lenten season, we have reflected upon our sins and chosen an appropriate fasting regimen. We have begun to work with it on Ash Wednesday. This week, we commit to it fully. This week, too, we should begin the work of regular charitable giving.

The Gospel

The Gospel for this week comes from Matthew, Chapter 4, verses 1–11:

> At that time, Jesus was led by the Spirit into the desert, to be tempted by the devil. And when he had fasted forty days and forty nights, afterwards he was hungry. And the tempter coming said to him: "If thou be the Son of God, command that these stones be made bread." Who answered and said: "It is written, Not in bread alone doth man live, but in every word that proceedeth from the mouth of God."
>
> Then the devil took him up into the holy city, and set him upon the pinnacle of the temple, And said to him: "If thou be the Son of God, cast thyself down, for it is written: That he hath given his angels charge over thee, and in their hands shall they bear thee up, lest perhaps thou dash thy foot against a stone."
>
> Jesus said to him: "It is written again: Thou shalt not tempt the Lord thy God."
>
> Again, the devil took him up into a very high mountain, and shewed him all the kingdoms of the world, and the glory of them, And said to him: "All these will I give thee, if falling down thou wilt adore me." Then Jesus saith to him: "Begone, Satan: for it is written: The Lord thy God shalt thou adore, and him only shalt thou serve."
>
> Then the devil left him, and behold, angels came and ministered to him.

Themes of the first week of Lent

The great image of this week, which begins Lent and which will remain with us throughout the season, is the *temptation of Christ in the desert*.

Imagine the scene. Christ has just undergone his baptism by John, and the Holy Spirit has descended upon him. Now he goes into retreat in the wilderness to fast and pray.

We will often see that particular episodes from the Gospels act like microcosms or "condensed versions" of the Christian story as a whole, or of particular aspects of it. In this case, the entire story is a model in miniature of the way of initiation. We begin with the baptism and the descent of the Holy Spirit. This parallels the initial rush of joy, excitement, and spiritual energy that we feel at the beginning of any work of initiation. Everyone who has begun a spiritual practice of any kind knows this feeling, and very often those who begin other sorts of practices as well. A person who has begun running, learning to cook, or even writing a book experiences this.

But after the Holy Spirit inevitably comes the wandering in the desert. In the work of initiation, this is the discovery that initiation takes *work*. It isn't long before that first rush of excitement wears off, and the surge of spiritual energy eventually dies back. The mind begins to ask, "Do I really have to sit down and practice this meditation every day?" And the world very quickly replies, "Of course not!" and then offers countless distractions. This is the temptation in the desert, and it is a natural part of every spiritual practice and, indeed, of every attempt which human beings make to accomplish anything or to improve their lives.

In the spiritual life, this is also known as *dryness* or *desolation*, terms which calls to mind the emptiness that Our Lord would have found in the desert. In the Christian liturgical year, this *is* the season of Lent, which comes after the initial rush of excitement and renewal during the Christmas season and the great joy of the Easter season. In the Mysteries of the Rosary, the same pattern is found, and this is why the Sorrowful Mysteries come after the Joyful Mysteries and before the Glorious Mysteries.

And so we see that, during Lent, we are in the middle phase of a threefold process of initiation. We began, in joy, at Christmas; we will complete our work in glory at Easter and Pentecost. In between, we must wander in the wilderness and face down the temptations of the Devil. Do not turn aside! Do not set down your burden! Glory awaits at the end of the road.

There are three additional themes associated with this Sunday, and these should inform your practice and your meditation in the week to come.

The first is the theme of *renewal*. This is the First Sunday, and, as we have said, it is symbolically the First Day of Creation. *Let there be light*. This week in your meditations, focus on the idea that you have withdrawn from the world and from your personal world in order that you, and your world, may be re-created in a manner in harmony with the Divine Will for you and for your life.

The second theme is the theme of *repentance*. This is Brand Sunday, when the youths present themselves at the church on Sunday morning. Nor do they sneak in through a side door and hide behind a column. No: They turn up at the front door with a torch burning, unmistakable. Each of us has the wild young person in our soul, and this is the part that easily gives in to the passions, to temptation, and to sin. This week, if you haven't already, begin to take inventory of your sins and begin to work with the Reconciliation practice.

The third theme can simply be called reliance on God, and this takes two forms. In the first case, as in the Introit to today's Mass, we call upon God and rely on Him to fill us. We have withdrawn from the comforts of the material world, from its pleasures and its distractions. Now we turn to God alone as the source of our sustenance, and we trust that we will be filled.

It is not enough, however, simply to focus on ourselves. It is one of the great teachings of the spiritual life that, if we want to invoke any energy into ourselves, we must attune ourselves to it. We wish to be filled by God and to rely on him for our sustenance. We can aid in this process by becoming like God insofar as possible. Thus, we begin the work of giving and charity: God is an ever-flowing fountain of life, and if we would partake of those waters we must become a channel of them ourselves. We must give, that we may be like our Father in Heaven, and we may trust that in so doing we shall receive.

Practice for the first week of Lent

Every week, preferably on Sunday, we are going to enter into an open temple and meditate on the Gospel.

The first time you do this, do your best to visualize the scene as clearly as possible. Allow yourself to enter as deeply into the experience as possible. Imagine you are with Jesus, feeling what he feels, seeing what he sees. Feel the heat of the desert Sun during the day, and the cold of the night. Feel the pangs of hunger and thirst, and feel yourself resist them.

At last, see the Devil appear. He has three temptations to offer, to you just as to Our Lord: The first is the temptation to submit to the demands of the body, despite your commitment to the spiritual life.

The second is the temptation to abuse the powers of magic, the mind, and the spiritual life, either for the sake of power or frivolity. The third is the temptation to worldly authority, provided you reject the spiritual life and commit yourself to the world.

Consider these temptations seriously and what they mean in your life. If you find that you are unable, at this time, to reject them, don't condemn yourself, but simply take note of this fact. Pray for the grace to live a holier life.

When you have concluded your meditations, rise and offer the following prayer:

> Deliver me, Oh Lord, from all evil,
> And from all temptations of the Devil.
> May I walk with thee on this Lenten journey,
> And may my soul be created anew in the light of Thy Truth.

In the days that follow, you may take the themes for your meditation from the Gospel, the relevant passage from Genesis, or the discussion of the themes of this week.

Spring Ember Days

The Ember Days are special fasts linked with the four seasons of the year. Ember Days are three-day fasts, falling on a Wednesday, Friday, and Saturday. The Spring Ember Days fall during the first full week of Lent—that is, after the First Sunday—and thus their exact date varies somewhat widely from year to year.

As noted in the introduction to this book, I've decided to keep most of the feasts and fasts not directly related to Lent for another book. The Ember fast, however, is a part of the season of Lent, and keeping it will allow us to continue the work of connection with the elements that we began at Christmastime.

The element of Air

As Winter is associated with the element of Earth, Spring is associated with the element of Air.

Air is understood as heat and moisture, the second most subtle of the elements, after Fire. Air also has the following associations:

Among times, the Dawn; infancy in a lifetime; the mind in man; atmosphere, weather, and wind in nature; the flower in plants, and seeds born on the wind, and also all such plants as dwell in the air; among herbs, all those hot and moist by temperament; among animals, birds and all flying creatures; among professions, those related to the Air, including pilots, astronomers, meteorologists, and all those who work with their minds, or who make their living by communication; in society, it is the economy and all means of transportation, production, and exchange; among planets, it is Jupiter and Mercury, though others say the Sun; among numbers, the number 2 and all its permutations; among solids, the octahedron.

Every element is ruled by an archangel. It's worth taking a moment to consider the meaning of the word "angel." The word means "messenger." Saint Augustine tells us that "angels" is their title; their nature is spirit. In the Christian tradition, mainstream as well as esoteric, they are given the government of the physical world and human society. At the same time, they are called "messengers." This is a bit of a paradox—you wouldn't give the president of a country the title of "chief mailman." So what is going on here?

The resolution of the paradox is this: The angels govern the elements of the material world and the universe as a whole as an expression of the Divine Will. In earlier times, it was said that the whole of Nature was one of two books written by the Holy Ghost; as such, all of creation is a kind of message from God. And the angels that govern creation are the message-bearers.

The Ember Fast

This week, extend whatever fasting commitment you've made to Wednesday, Friday, and Saturday. In addition, make at least one additional effort toward lightening your impact on the Earth. You might make an effort to reduce your own contribution to air pollution. As Air rules the system of economic exchange in society, you might keep a closer watch on your spending this week, and try to support local businesses and those which follow sound environmental practices. On at least one of these days, spend some additional time in Nature. Allow yourself to be aware of the Air element as it manifests in the wind and the atmosphere and in everything that is in motion, as well as those creatures that are specifically governed by it. You might also consider donating to an Air-oriented charity, such as an organization dedicated to helping children learn to read or speak, or any organization dedicated to bird conservation.

At least once during the Ember Days, or all three days if you like, practice the following meditation:

The Spring Ember Days meditation

Preparation. For the sake of this meditation only, you may use a yellow or gold cloth for your altar. You may wish to include other images associated with air or Springtime, such as flowers, a feather, or even a notebook and pen (given Air's association with communication and the mind). You may also wish to include an image of the archangel Raphael and a yellow candle.

Step 1. Open the temple as you have been instructed.

Step 3. Rise, and with hands in the orans posture, pray the prayer of the Holy Spirit:

> Come, Holy Spirit, fill the hearts of Thy faithful and enkindle in them the fire of Thy love.
>
> Send forth Thy Spirit and they shall be created, and Thou shalt renew the face of the earth.
>
> Let us pray.
>
> O God, Who didst instruct the hearts of the faithful by the light of the Holy Spirit, grant us in the same Spirit to be truly wise, and ever to rejoice in His consolation, through Christ, our Lord. Amen.

Step 4. Kneeling or seated, take a few moments to relax your body and clear your mind with rhythmic breathing. Then call to mind the Air element and the Spring season, and everything pertaining to them. Offer a prayer, such as the following:

> Oh God, I thank thee for all the gifts of the element of Air. For movement and change, the lengthening days and the Spring rains, and all the gifts of the air and the mental world. And I pray that thou wilt send thy holy archangel Raphael, who governs the element of Air, to be with us at this time. Holy Saint Raphael, archangel who governs the element of Air, grant that the gifts and virtues of Air, willingness and wisdom, honesty and lightness of

spirit may be manifest in our lives. And grant, too, that the unbalanced manifestations of Air, including concupiscence, dishonesty and unreliability, may be kept far from us. Through Jesus Christ our Lord. Amen.

Step 5. Take a moment to visualize the gifts and virtues of Air manifesting in your life and the lives of your family members and loved ones. Then close your meditation with rhythmic breathing.

Step 6. Close your temple as you have been instructed.

The Second Sunday of Lent

The Second Sunday of Lent is known as Transfiguration Sunday, or, alternatively, as Reminiscere Sunday. As always, the Latin name comes from the Introit to the Mass, which today reads as follows:

> *Reminiscere miserationum tuarum, Domine, et misericordiae tuæ, quae a saeculo sunt: ne unquam dominentur nobis inimici nostri: libera nos, Deus Israel, ex omnibus angustiis nostris.*
>
> Remember, O Lord, thy tender mercies and thy compassion of old, that my enemies may never rule over us. Deliver us from all our distress, O God of Israel.

The name of Transfiguration Sunday comes from the Gospel, which consists, fittingly enough, of Matthew's account of the Transfiguration. We will come to that shortly, when we consider the Gospel in detail.

Genesis

This Sunday is the second day, the day on which God said, Let there be light.

> And God said, Let there be a firmament in the midst of the waters, and let it divide the waters from the waters. And God made the firmament, and divided the waters which were under the firmament from the waters which were above the firmament: and it was so. And God called the firmament Heaven. And the evening and the morning were the second day.

This is one of those passages which can be difficult for modern people to reconcile. Part of the problem, of course, is simply that the people who compiled the Book of Genesis were working with a radically different cosmology from our own. We live in a time of giant telescopes and space probes, and we're well aware that there isn't a literal firmament separating our ocean from another ocean somewhere above our heads. Knowing this, we're often tempted simply to dismiss this part of the Scriptures as "outdated" and ignore it. Meanwhile, our time has also seen the development of "literal" interpretations of the Scriptures, which attempt to insist, in the teeth of all evidence, that the story of Genesis ought to be treated as an ancient work of journalism.

For our purposes here, neither of these approaches is helpful. Instead, we need to consider the symbolic meaning: What is water, from a magical perspective? What is the firmament intended to separate?

Now, among the Four Elements, Water is the symbol of the Soul. And the Soul, in the esoteric tradition, has two modes of existence. There is the Universal Soul, and there are the particular souls of individuals, which derive their existence from the Universal Soul. Among individual souls, meanwhile, there are those which are contained within bodies and those which are not. The firmament can be said to divide both of these. The Waters above the Heavens refers, then, both to the Universal Soul which is uncontained by any body, and to the particular souls of those exalted beings who abide beyond material incarnation. The firmament divides the collective soul of our material world from the world above. Our own state, incarnate in human bodies, is an image of this soul, contained within the firmament.

But what shall we contain? The firmament is a limit, or a barrier. The endless waters above the Heavens contain infinite possibilities. In order, however, for anything to come into being, a barrier must be created so that some of those possibilities may become actualities. The same is true in our own lives. We cannot be at once a doctor, a soldier, a monk, a baker, and a CEO; some of these possibilities must be chosen, others set aside, either for good or simply for a later time. And we also cannot be at once a faithful partner and an adulterer, a good or a negligent parent, a citizen or a traitor, a follower of the law or a criminal. Some of these must be chosen, others must be firmly rejected.

In our meditation this week, we should consider the role of barriers and limits like this in our own lives. What are our goals, and what are our responsibilities? What should be set aside, and what must be set aside?

There are two other ways that we can think of the firmament, and it will be helpful if we can hold both of these in our minds.

The classical and medieval worlds saw the universe as a system of spheres surrounding the Earth. The last of the spheres was the sphere of the Fixed Stars, which contained the entirety of the material world.

In the work of Plato and of his predecessor Empedocles, the material world is envisioned as a cave. Hold this image in your mind, and remember that the ancient Christians saw the manger in which Christ was born as a cave—and remember, too, that it is in a cave that he will be laid after His death on Good Friday. The cave of Plato is also a prison, in which we are trapped, and a crypt in which we are entombed.

The church father Origen noted that the firmament separated the waters above from the waters below. Now, Water is associated with two rather different images. On the one hand, Water is an image of the primordial chaos that we encountered on Ash Wednesday and in the opening lines of the First Book of Genesis: darkness was upon the face of the Deep. On the other hand, Water is also the symbol of life and of the soul itself, and Our Lord Himself is the font of the water of life.

And so the firmament is at once a force which separates heavenly water, or life, from the chaos of the waters below; a tomb and a cave, in which we are buried or imprisoned; a limiting force which allows us to live and grow according to God's purpose for us. These images are different and appear to contradict one another. Rather than trying to resolve the contradiction, simply try to hold them all together in your mind.

The Gospel

The Gospel for this week comes from Matthew, Chapter 4, verses 1–11:

> At that time, Jesus taketh unto him Peter and James, and John his brother, and bringeth them up into a high mountain apart: And he was transfigured before them. And his face did shine as the sun: and his garments became white as snow. And behold there appeared to them Moses and Elias talking with him. And Peter answering, said to Jesus: Lord, it is good for us to be here: if thou wilt, let us make here three tabernacles, one for thee, and one for Moses, and one for Elias.
>
> And as he was yet speaking, behold a bright cloud overshadowed them. And lo a voice out of the cloud, saying: "This is my

beloved Son, in whom I am well pleased: hear ye him." And the disciples hearing fell upon their face, and were very much afraid. And Jesus came and touched them: and said to them: "Arise, and fear not." And they lifted up their eyes, saw no one, but only Jesus.

And as they came down from the mountain, Jesus charged them, saying: "Tell the vision to no man, till the Son of man be risen from the dead."

Themes of the second week of Lent

The great image of this week, given to us both to understand the purpose of our Lenten work and to inspire us to perseverance, is the *Transfiguration of Christ*.

Again, let us consider the scene. The first thing we notice is that it takes place on a mountaintop. Now, the esoteric tradition teaches us that all visible things in the material world are reflections of eternal things in the spiritual world. Everything in the world of Nature is a reflection, at the level of the visible and tangible, of ideas which are invisible and beyond the physical world.

From that perspective, what is a mountain? In Nature, it is a structure of the physical earth which rises toward the sky. As an idea, then, a mountain represents the material world, and those of us who live in material bodies, reaching toward the eternal, celestial world.

This is why, throughout the world and in all religious traditions, mountains are places of initiation, transformation, and encounter with the Divine. Moses receives the Ten Commandments on Mount Sinai. The gods dwell on Mount Olympus. Japan has the Three Holy Mountains of Fuji, Tateyama, and Hakusan. No one honors a swamp or a meadow in this way—though they may honor them in other ways—because the symbolism of a swamp is different.

The Transfiguration takes place on a mountain. Now, mountains in mythology are like trees; they are images of the *axis mundi*, the vertical pole that holds the many worlds together. The top of the mountain is Heaven, and is always the dwelling place of the gods. Indeed, sacred mountains can be found the world over, from Athos in Greece to Fuji in Japan, and people who have climbed mountains know well that spiritual forces may be encountered there. Like all things in our material world, mountains are a visible image of an eternal spiritual reality.

And what do the Disciples encounter, then, at the top of the mountain, in the place of the gods?

Christ transfigured, shining like the Sun, and the saints coming forth to discourse with him. This is a vision of Heaven, and it is also a vision of the Communion of Saints.

The nature of the pagan gods has been much disputed in Christian circles over the centuries. At times, they were simply seen as lesser powers or angels, or perhaps as great men and women who were worshipped after their death. At other times, they were seen as evil powers or demons. In our own time, desperate to avoid the appearance of saying anything interesting, many mainstream Christian denominations simply deny their existence and suppose that human beings the world over have simply been deluded when they described encounters with them.

As is often the case, a better understanding emerges if we consider multiple possibilities at once.

Plato, Aristotle, and many other philosophers and sages of the ancient world were honored by early Christians and were even seen to have been inspired by angels. The view that I'm presenting in this book takes this idea further, of course, but you don't have to accept that. You can simply look at icons in Orthodox churches depicting Plato, Aristotle, Socrates, Homer, and others. They are depicted without halos as the Orthodox don't feel that it's appropriate to offer them veneration (I disagree), but they are there. And they were pagans: When Aristotle spoke of God as the First Cause and Unmoved Mover; when Plato spoke of God as the all-good Creator who had made the material world and all of the gods of the Greeks, they had the stories of Zeus and the Olympians in their minds. Evil cannot produce good, and demons cannot elevate the mind to the contemplation of the Eternal Good.

At the same time, no one who has studied ancient paganism is unaware that the gods could be capricious, spiteful, cruel and jealous. Their stories were often quite gruesome, and this gruesomeness could be carried over into their worship. Plato himself wrote (not with approval) of the prevalence of human sacrifice in his time in certain parts of the world. (see Laws: Something).

So what is going on here?

Here is a way to think about it. According to the old Neoplatonic view, everything begins with God, the first cause, who can be thought of as like a point at the center of the circle. From that point, spokes radiate outward in every direction until finally they reach the circumference of the circle, which is our material world. God is found at every point along the spokes, but so are other beings. The further removed from God Himself they are, the less they participate in His goodness. Evil itself has no true existence, but is only the absence of Good, as dark has no power of its own but is only the absence of light. Every one of those spokes that radiates from the center, however, has its own nature and its own particular qualities, and each type of being along each spoke will also have those sorts of qualities. One spoke, for example, might represent God's love. Further out, this is embodied by archangels and angels who transmit God's love to the world. Further still might be intermediate beings, and finally earth-bound spirits. Among the earth-bound spirits, some will represent love at its lowest and most material form: This is the base craving for sexual gratification at all expense, and in our experience these manifest as demons of infidelity, rape, and worse. Very often, our ancestors took to worshipping the lowest of these beings and giving them the names of gods, until it seemed that all humanity was trapped under the rule of evil spirits. In Christian mythology, these are seen as rebel angels who have turned away from God, but I believe that these must be seen as myths. An angel cannot truly fall, but we can turn away from the good and toward the bad, and it can seem to us that this is so.

The Resurrection of Christ is the breaking of the power of the evil spirits, and here we are given an image of what that means. It is the nature of angelic beings to abide in the presence of God, but our nature is to descend into matter and to return, and when we do so, we too will be exalted, as are Moses and Elijah. It is a powerful image. Let us hold in our minds as a source of spiritual nourishment and inspiration that we persevere in the work of our Lenten pilgrimage.

Practice for the second week of Lent

On Sunday (or as early in the week as possible), open a temple and visualize the Transfiguration. Imagine yourself making your way up Mount Tabor with the Disciples, and then standing witness as Christ is revealed in his Glory and Moses and Elijah appear to speak with him. Consider in your meditations that this is an image of the spiritual journey as a whole, which you yourself have undertaken: The grueling climb up the mountain, which is the material world; standing in the clear air of the Heavenly world, in the light of the Eternal Sun; becoming transfigured, transformed in the light, your own true nature revealed. What is that true nature?

In the days that follow, you may take the themes for your meditation from the Gospel, the relevant passage from Genesis, or the discussion of the themes of this week. New thoughts, ideas, and connections will emerge as you work. Write these down in your meditation journal.

When you have concluded your meditations, rise and offer the following prayer:

> Let me be transformed, Oh Lord,
> And let me stand with thee in the light.
> Let the eternal nature within me be separated from the dark, turbid waters.

The Third Sunday of Lent

The Third Sunday of Lent is called Scrutiny Sunday, as this is when the Catachumens would begin to be examined, and Oculi Sunday, from the first words to the Introit:

> *Oculi mei semper ad Dominum, quia ipse evellet de laqueo pedes meos. Respice in me, et miserere mei, quoniam unicus et pauper sum ego.*

> My eyes are ever toward the Lord, for He shall free my feet from the snare. Look upon me, and have pity on me, for I am alone and wretched.

Genesis

On the Third Day, the waters of the Earth are gathered into the seas, and the Earth brings forth plants and trees, the vegetable creation:

> And God said, Let the waters under the heaven be gathered together unto one place, and let the dry land appear: and it was so. And God called the dry land Earth; and the gathering together of the waters called He seas: and God saw that it was good. And God said, Let the earth bring forth grass, the herb yielding seed, and the fruit tree yielding fruit after his kind, whose seed is in itself, upon the earth: and it was so.

There is much we can draw from this simple passage.

First, note that this is the beginning of the world of Nature in the sense that we know. The waters are now gathered into their own place, and for the first time, dry land emerges. And from the land, the first life appears, in the form of plants which yield seed and fruit, "each according to its own kind."

Note that this is a process of creation which will culminate in the creation of human beings. In another sense, as we will learn in Genesis 3, human beings were created before the material world, but our form does not appear until after all things have been created. Thus, we can truly understand that our creation is the completion of the work of creation. Note that Christ is called the True Adam, that is, the true Human Being, and remember (we shall encounter them again) his last words on the Cross: "It is accomplished." It? What? Nothing other than the Creation of the world, which is finally complete on the Seventh Day, that is, Easter Sunday.

For now, note that the first living beings on the Earth are the herbs and trees of the vegetable creation.

We have already seen that Plato divided the soul into three parts, called the *nous, thymos,* and *epithymia.* Aristotle, his wayward follower, also divided the soul into three, but he understood them somewhat differently. The two views do not actually contradict but complement one another, and it's the Aristotelian view that I want to discuss now.

The rational soul resides in the head; it consists of the capacity to think and reason, and at its highest level, to see into the spiritual world. This is found in human beings and perhaps some animals (storks, the ancients thought, though modern people are more likely to think of dolphins or bonobos), and to a lesser extent in other animals. The vital soul is shared by humans and all animals; its seat in our bodies is in the chest, and it governs our vitality and our capacity for movement. The Vegetable Soul is shared by all living things. In human beings, it resides in the abdomen, and it governs our capacity for growth, assimilation (and excretion) of food, and reproduction.

The Vegetable Soul is closely linked with Nature. Nature, in this sense, also has a technical definition. It doesn't just mean "the woods" or "the outdoors." Instead, it refers to the capacity of things to both remain as they are and to change and reproduce themselves. The difference between artificial and natural things is found precisely in the fact that artificial things can only decay over time: they don't repair themselves, and they don't make more of themselves. Cut down a tree and bury it, and another tree will grow out of its stump; knock down a house, and another house will never grow out of the foundation, unless someone comes along and builds one.

Thus, Nature and the Vegetable Soul are prior to human beings and the rest of God's Creation, and everything that follows from them shares in their powers. We all have the Vegetable Soul within us—if we didn't, we couldn't make babies or digest food. And we all have a nature. We have a nature as human beings, as men or women, and each of us has our own nature as individuals.

The Third Sunday of Lent, then, is a good time to reflect on our natures, and on Nature as a whole. If we have a nature, it is intimately linked with God's purpose for us, as he has created the microcosm of our individual selves just as he created the macrocosm of the entire world. What is the purpose for which you were created? What are you good at, toward what are you naturally inclined, and toward what are you drawn, whether you will or no?

In this way, we participate in the tradition of the Scrutiny. We will continue to discuss this in even more detail later, when we come to this week's Gospel.

This week is also a good time to deepen our connection with the wider world of Nature, if you haven't begun to do so already. Much of our lives is spent in artificial environments. It isn't "wrong" to live in a house or have air conditioning or even to use a cell phone (with moderation), but it isn't the work of God either. The more time we can spend in the living world, among natural things, the better we will be for it.

The Gospel

> At that time, Jesus was casting out a devil: and the same was dumb. And when he had cast out the devil, the dumb spoke: and the multitudes were in admiration at it. But some of them said: "He casteth out devils by Beelzebub, the prince of devils." And others, tempting, asked of him a sign from heaven. But he, seeing their thoughts, said to them: "Every kingdom divided against itself shall be brought to desolation; and house upon house shall fall. And if Satan also be divided against himself, how shall his kingdom stand? Because you say that through Beelzebub I cast out devils. Now if I cast out devils by Beelzebub, by whom do your children cast them out?

Therefore, they shall be your judges. But if I by the finger of God cast out devils, doubtless the kingdom of God is come upon you. When a strong man armed keepeth his court, those things are in peace which he possesseth. But if a stronger than he come upon him and overcome him, he will take away all his armour wherein he trusted and will distribute his spoils. He that is not with me is against me; and he that gathereth not with me scattereth. When the unclean spirit is gone out of a man, he walketh through places without water, seeking rest: and not finding, he saith: I will return into my house whence I came out. And when he is come, he findeth it swept and garnished. Then he goeth and taketh with him seven other spirits more wicked than himself: and entering in they dwell there. And the last state of that man becomes worse than the first."

And it came to pass, as he spoke these things, a certain woman from the crowd, lifting up her voice, said to him: "Blessed is the womb that bore thee and the paps that gave thee suck." But he said: "Yea rather, blessed are they who hear the Word of God and keep it."

Themes of the third week of Lent

The Gospel for this week is short, but it contains a set of themes critical to our spiritual development.

We begin with Our Lord at what is, in truth, his usual work: The casting out of demons. Exorcism is downplayed in modern culture, relegated, largely, to horror movies and to certain subcultures within the Christian churches. When Jesus's ministry is spoken of in popular culture, we usually hear about his compassion and his teachings regarding the poor, as though he had primarily come to create a registered nonprofit. And yet, if we examine the Gospels, we find that they are filled with stories of exorcism. The synoptic Gospels contain more than 60 stories of exorcism. Mark makes an exorcism, Jesus's first major act after receiving his initiation from John and gathering the first of his disciples.

In our Gospel today, he begins by driving an evil spirit out of a man. The Pharisees, seeing this, promptly accuse Him of demonolatry: "He casts out demons by Beelzebub, the prince of the demons." This gives Him an opportunity to teach us something about the spiritual life and something about the nature of the soul. The same story, by the way, is also found in Mark 3:23–27 and in Luke 11:17–22. It's worth setting the three passages side by side, as together they make the same point.

From all of these, we can draw a series of ideas.

First, if an exorcism is truly performed by an evil power, it will not work. It is possible that there may, for a time, seem to have been results, with the evil spirit seemingly driven forth. Before very long, however, the situation will grow worse, as the first demon gathers "seven spirits more wicked than himself," so that the state of the soul is worse in the end than in the beginning. And this is because, ultimately, Satan *cannot* cast out Satan.

Evil, as we have said before, has no true reality. In this world of shadows, it may seem that evil has power. The truth is that only God is power, as well as goodness and existence itself: And ultimately these things are one thing, one light shining from the face of God. Evil spirits are teetering on the very edge of nonexistence, and only here in the world below do they seem to have any power at all. Satan can no more cast out Satan than a shadow can lighten a room: to even suggest it is an absurdity.

There is an obvious corollary to this.

In Jesus's time, it seems, the effects of demonic activity included such things as muteness, paralysis, and insanity. In our own time, we are far more likely to see its results in such things as drug abuse, alcoholism, sexual addiction, and so on: patterns of compulsive behavior that result in the destruction of the souls of individuals, families, and entire communities. It follows that anything which truly cures these things is of God, whether or not it is of any particular church or doctrine. I once knew a man who had been a severe heroin addict. He spent 18 months at a Buddhist monastery in India and was cured; after this time, the condition of his soul was better and not worse. If this is the case, it must be the case that the demon of heroin addiction was cast out by God, as it could not have been cast out by Satan.

After this, we're given a verse which has been much abused in the last five centuries or so. Being told, "Blessed is the womb that bore you," Jesus replies, "Rather, blessed are they who hear the Word of God and keep it." Rather tragically, this verse, like several others, has been used as a weapon in the hands of those who wish to destroy the cult of the Virgin Mary. If we consider the matter further, this makes very little sense. Much earlier in the Gospels, we have already learned from Mary herself that "from henceforth all generations shall call Her blessed." This occurred during her visit to Elizabeth and in reply to the words, "blessed art thou among women, and blessed is the fruit of thy womb."

But notice when this episode takes place: Only once Mary has fully assented to the Will of God: "Behold the handmaiden of the Lord: Be it done unto me according to Thy Word."

Blessed are they that hear the Word of God and keep it: This is what we are truly being taught here. The era since Christ's birth is the era of the re-making of the world, or, in another sense, of the true completion of the Creation. In the Christian era, Mary was the first of those who heard the Word of God and kept it: Thus she is the first among the Blessed, that is, the saints, and she shows the path that the rest of us are to follow.

Practice for the third week of Lent

Once again, open your temple in the usual way, read and visualize the Gospel scene. Imagine the demoniac, and see Christ drive the demon from him. Imagine the crowds, confused about the source of Jesus's power. Consider the meaning of His words when he tells us that, if the demon is simply driven out, it will soon return, "with seven other spirits more wicked than himself," so that "the last state of that man becomes worse than the first." And consider the immediate follow-up: "Blessed are they that blessed are they who hear the Word of God and keep it."

Each of us has our own besetting devils, our patterns of habitual sin, some learned on our own, others inherited from our families or our cultures. The work of overcoming these is not simply a work of abstinence from sin but of connection with God. To hear and keep the Word of God is to unite ourselves with the Divine Will.

Note that this Gospel recapitulates the themes of the previous two, condensed into one. In the first week, we encountered the temptation of the Devil; in the second, we saw the fruits of the spiritual journey in the Transfiguration. Now we consider both of these themes together. What sins and what ingrained habits of behavior keep you from your true self, the life for which God created you? In what ways can you better "hear the Word of God, and keep it"?

When you have concluded your meditations, rise and offer the following prayer:

> Thou hast cast out the darkness, Oh Lord,
> And thou hast given life to the Earth.
> Drive forth from me all darkness,
> And come to reign in my soul.

In the days that follow, you may take the themes for your meditation from the Gospel, the relevant passage from Genesis, or the discussion of the themes of this week.

Mid-Lent and the Burial of Winter

The period from the Wednesday of the third week of Lent to the Wednesday of the fourth week is called Mid-Lent. Mid-Lent is a time of celebration amid the Lenten rigors. The center of this time is Laetare Sunday, which is the Sunday of the Fourth Week. As Laetare Sunday has its own special practices, we will present the symbolism and practices of Mid-Lent here. Be aware that you can work with this material at any time between this Wednesday and next Wednesday.

Mid-Lent is especially associated with the end of Winter and the coming of Spring. At this point, the days have begun to visibly lengthen. Often, Mid-Lent will fall after the Spring Equinox. Invariably, it will fall after February 2, Candlemas and Saint Brigid's Day, which is another date from which the beginning of Spring is marked.

One of the most interesting customs of this season is the Burial of Winter, practiced in German and Slavic countries. On this occasion, an effigy representing Winter, or Death, is paraded through the town and then either burned or drowned. For this reason, Laetare Sunday also had the name of "Dead Sunday" in parts of Germany.

In parts of France and Italy, the day has the rather more upbeat name of *Fontana*, which refers to the decorating of wells and fountains with flowers and branches. Water sources such as wells have been sacred places, hallowed to the gods and potentially gateways to the Otherworld of the spirits, since pre-Christian times. Following the coming of Christianity, the sacred wells remained, but now received a saint or the Blessed Virgin as their guardian.

It is customary in many regions to celebrate Mid-Lent with a festive meal at home. Laetare Sunday itself is best if you wish to keep this practice (as Sundays are free from fasting), but you may follow your own inner guidance and the demands of your schedule in this matter.

This is also a traditional time for matchmaking and the announcement of engagements. Note that this is not the time for weddings, but for proposals. This fits the symbolism of the beginning of life at this time, but not its full flowering.

Practice for Mid-Lent

As the customs of Mid-Lent are varied, the exact way that you celebrate it is up to you, and it can be simple or elaborate. At a minimum, you might place flowers on your altar between the two Wednesdays. You may wish to host a dinner party or share a special meal with your family. The countries of the Western hemisphere are unfortunately limited in their number of sacred wells, but most of us live near some natural body of water—a spring, stream or creek. You can connect with the symbolism of the Fontana celebrations by making your way to your favorite local water source, casting flowers or branches into it and saying a prayer of blessing over it.

It is, moreover, a good time to re-connect with Nature as a whole.

Finally, in connection with the Burial of Winter, you may perform the following simple practice.

The Burial of Winter

You will need to start by creating an image of Winter. Do this on paper, so that you can burn it when you are finished. What the image looks like is up to you. You may draw a traditional image of Death, with his black hood and scythe, and surround it with images of snow and ice, or you might draw an image of a snow queen (or king), or a similar type of nature spirit, representing Winter's cold. If you like, you can deepen the work by turning the paper over and writing down all those aspects of Winter which you hope to release—any Winter depression or doldrums, apathy, or inactivity, or whatever makes sense to you. You can then write down your hopes for the coming Spring.

This is the type of practice that children often enjoy, and so you can feel free to involve your family. When you are ready, say the following prayer:

> We give thanks to God and to the spirits of Winter for the gifts we have received in these cold months, and we release [here name any specific things you wish to let go of.] May God and his saints, and the spirits of Spring, watch over and guide us in the season to come and help us to [name those things you hope to achieve in the Spring.] We ask this through Jesus Christ, Our Lord. Amen.

Feel free to modify the language, especially when you are working with a group that includes children or people who simply aren't used to this sort of thing.

Proceed together to an outdoor place where you can burn the image. (If that is impossible, you can tear it into pieces and bury it, or place it into running water and let the current carry it away.)

As you do so, say the following prayer—again, feel free to modify or omit this, as it suits your needs:

> In Winter, all things slumber and die, but Hope is born again in the darkness.
> O Death, where is thy sting? O Grave, where is thy victory?
> In Spring, all things awaken and live again, and Hope triumphs over Death:
> In Christ all things are made new.

Following this is a perfect time to celebrate with a meal or a small party.

The Fourth Sunday of Lent

The Fourth Sunday in Lent is called Laetare Sunday, after the first words to the Introit, and also Rose Sunday, for reasons we shall come to presently.

> *Laetare, Jerusalem: Et conventum facite. omnes qui diligitis eam. Gaudete cum laetitia, qui in tristitia fuistis: ut exsultetis, et satiemini ab uberibus consolationis vestrae.*
>
> Rejoice, O Jerusalem, and come together all you who love her. Rejoice with joy, you who have been in sorrow, that you may exalt, and be filled from the abundance of your consolation.

On the Third Sunday of Advent, the rose candle is lit. The other three candles of the Advent wreath are purple, the symbol of penitence, but the rose candle is a symbol of joy and a foretaste of the Christmas feast to come.

In the same way, the Fourth Sunday of Lent is Rose Sunday, a time of rejoicing in the midst of the penitential season and a foretaste of the joy of Easter.

On Rose Sunday, a golden rose is blessed by the Pope and then conferred upon a particular church. The origins of the custom are unknown, but it apparently is quite ancient, as popes 1000 years ago described it as an "ancient custom." The rose is blessed that the people of God "may with sincere hearts show forth their joy" this day.

> Wherefore, O Lord, on this day, when the Church exults in Thy name and manifests her joy by this sign, confer upon us through her true and perfect joy and accepting her devotion of today; do Thou remit sin, strengthen faith, increase piety, protect her in Thy mercy, drive away all things adverse to her and make her ways safe and prosperous, so that Thy Church, as the fruit of good works, may unite in giving forth the perfume of the ointment of that flower sprung from the root of Jesse and which is the mystical flower of the field and lily of the valleys, and remain happy without end in eternal glory together with all the saints.

The rose is an important symbol in Western spiritual traditions, similar in its way to the role played by the lotus in the East. It is the symbol of the heart, of joy, and of love. Remember that the three spiritual virtues are faith, hope, and love, and that, as Saint Paul has taught us, "of these the most important is love."

Later in this chapter, we will look more at the rose and provide a meditation whereby we may connect with its spiritual energies. Now, on this fourth Sunday of Lent, let us look to the Fourth Day of Creation.

Genesis

> And God said, Let there be lights in the firmament of the heaven to divide the day from the night; and let them be for signs, and for seasons, and for days, and years: And let them be for lights in the firmament of the heaven to give light upon the earth: and it was so. And God made two great lights; the greater light to rule the day, and the lesser light to rule the night: he made the stars also. And God set them in the firmament of the heaven to give light upon the earth. And to rule over the day and over the night, and to divide the light from the darkness: and God saw that it was good.

On this day, we see the creation of the Sun and Moon and of the stars, which are given to rule over the day and the night.

The word "rule" here is not metaphorical. In ancient times, among Jews as well as gentiles, the lights in the Heavens were understood to be the visible bodies of invisible spiritual beings who govern the world. The exact nature of these beings changes from tradition to tradition. In the Jewish and Christian traditions, we usually use the word "angels" to describe them. The Bible does not, in fact, shy away from calling the lesser spiritual powers "gods," but it also makes it clear that all the gods are gathered under God Most High, who is their Creator as well as ours. The Sun rules the day, the Moon rules the night, and the stars are for signs and seasons.

Remember that the first non-Jews to come to worship Jesus, shortly after his birth, were Persian astrologers who followed a star to Bethlehem and were persecuted after. In the Gospel, it is Herod, and not the magi, who are condemned. And we know now from the work of archaeologists in the Holy Land that the synagogues in Galilee in Jesus's time were all painted with depictions of the 12 signs of the Zodiac. Our Lord Himself would have encountered astrology on a daily basis: But it was the bankers he chased from the temple, and not the astrologers.

This idea repeated elsewhere in the Old Testament, in Psalm 19, for example:

> The heavens declare the glory of God; and the firmament sheweth his handywork.
> Day unto day uttereth speech, and night unto night sheweth knowledge.
> There is no speech nor language, where their voice is not heard. Their line is gone out through all the earth, and their words to the end of the world. In them hath he set a tabernacle for the sun, Which is as a bridegroom coming out of his chamber, and rejoiceth as a strong man to run a race.

The "Heavens" which "proclaim the glory of God" are the stars, or, rather, the heavenly powers which dwell in the visible stars. And there is no speech or language where their voice is not heard. They are true gods, creations of God Most High, given charge of the material Earth.

But what is it that they do?

They "proclaim the glory of God." Elsewhere, in the Song of the Three Holy Youths, from the Book of Daniel, we read these words:

> O ye sun and moon, bless ye the Lord:
> Praise and exalt him above all for ever.

LENT 91

> O ye stars of heaven, bless ye the Lord:
> Praise and exalt him above all for ever.
> O every shower and dew, bless ye the Lord:
> Praise and exalt him above all for ever.
> O all ye winds, bless ye the Lord:
> Praise and exalt him above all for ever.
> O ye fire and heat, bless ye the Lord:
> Praise and exalt him above all for ever.
> O ye Winter and summer, bless ye the Lord:
> Praise and exalt him above all for ever.
> O ye dews and storms of snow, bless ye the Lord:
> Praise and exalt him above all for ever.
> O ye nights and days, bless ye the Lord:
> Praise and exalt him above all for ever ...

Again, these words are intended literally: The spiritual powers which govern the forces of nature bow to the One God, "bless the Lord," "praise and exalt him forever."

And yet, to return to Genesis, there is something strange about this passage, which is simply that it seems to portray the Sun and the stars as created after plant life, and after the Earth itself. From the perspective of our science, this is quite wrong, but, as we have already discussed, we aren't reading this either as a work of journalism or as a Geology textbook.

Nevertheless, even from a mythical or a spiritual perspective, it seems rather odd for the Sun and the stars to appear after the creation of plants. If the stars either are or are the images of exalted beings, gods or angels, how could they possibly come after plants in the order of creation?

The answer, of course, is that they could not, and did not. We have already seen the creation of "the Heavens and the Earth," of "Light and Darkness," and of "the firmament, called Heaven." The heavenly realm already exists and is already inhabited.

What does not exist, prior to the creation of the sorts of souls which inhabit bodies, is time.

Now, none of this ever happened, but all of it truly is. The stars as heavenly powers exist prior to the soul. But the soul, even in its vegetable form, exists in time: plants are born, they live, they die; they experience change and duration. Angels and heavenly powers act within time, or upon those beings who exist in time, but they have their own existence outside of it. It is only with the appearance of mortal souls that time has any meaning or any real existence. Only once the soul is there to experience change and duration do the Sun and the stars mark out times and seasons and days and years.

And so this must be a part of our meditations this week. Our lives, it is said, are marked out into seven periods, and each of these is governed by one of the seven wandering stars. The Moon governs us in our infancy; Mercury, in our childhood; Venus, in our youth; the Sun, in adulthood; Mars, in maturity; Jupiter, in middle age, and Saturn, in old age. The year, moreover, of the Sun is 365 days, but the year of Saturn—the time it takes for Saturn to make a complete revolution around the Sun—is 28 years. Saturn was the most distant planet known to the ancients, and so was considered the especial marker of Time itself. Many people do not make it past two years of Saturn, and few of us see three. What is it that we are doing with our time? How have the days of our youth shaped us in our maturity? It can be a very worthwhile exercise to mark out the phases of our life in intervals of seven years (a season of Saturn)—and to write down the things that happened to us, the things that we learned, and the things that we accomplished. In this way, we come to know ourselves, and we can set goals for the times to come.

The Gospel

> At that time, After these things Jesus went over the sea of Galilee, which is that of Tiberias. And a great multitude followed him, because they saw the miracles which he did on them that were diseased. Jesus therefore went up into a mountain: and there he sat with his disciples.
>
> Now the pasch, the festival day of the Jews, was near at hand. When Jesus therefore had lifted up his eyes and seen that a very great multitude cometh to him, he said to Philip: "Whence shall we buy bread, that these may eat?" And this he said to try him: for he himself knew what he would do.
>
> Philip answered him: "Two hundred pennyworth of bread is not sufficient for them that every one may take a little." One of his disciples, Andrew, the brother of Simon Peter, saith to him: "There is a boy here that hath five barley loaves and two fishes. But what are these among so many?" Then Jesus said: "Make the men sit down."

Now, there was much grass in the place. The men therefore sat down, in number about 5000. And Jesus took the loaves: and when he had given thanks, he distributed to them that were set down. In like manner also of the fishes, as much as they would. And when they were filled, he said to his disciples: "Gather up the fragments that remain, lest they be lost." They gathered up therefore and filled twelve baskets with the fragments of the five barley loaves which remained over and above to them that had eaten.

Now those men, when they had seen what a miracle Jesus had done, said: "This is of a truth the prophet that is to come into the world." Jesus therefore, when he knew that they would come to take him by force and make him king, fled again into the mountains, himself alone.

Themes of the fourth week of Lent

The Feeding of the Five Thousand! This is one of the great miracles of Christ's ministry, and it has an importance which has not always been understood.

Return to Genesis for a moment. As we have seen, the heavenly bodies can be seen as bodies or as statues, as they were sometimes called, of the gods who govern the world. God creates them, and sees that they are good, and sets them to certain tasks: to rule the day and night and to show forth events on Earth by their signs.

There is a difference, however, between "the gods" and "God." And that lies precisely in the fact that the gods, for all their exalted glory, are still created beings, while God is eternal and uncreated. This concept is not found only in Christianity. In his great dialogue *Timaeus*, Plato described God, the Creator of the Universe, forming the gods and setting them over the material universe. In *Timaeus* he addresses them in the following way:

> Gods, children of gods, who are my works, and of whom I am the artificer and father, my creations are indissoluble, if so I will. All that is bound may be undone, but only an evil being would wish to undo that which is harmonious and happy. Wherefore, since ye are but creatures, ye are not altogether immortal and indissoluble, but ye shall certainly not be dissolved, nor be liable to the fate of death ...

The "gods" described by Plato, then, are the same sorts of beings as those we usually know as "angels." Both names are acceptable: To call them "gods" tells us that they have a share in divinity, but they lack the simplicity and the oneness of God in the singular. To call them "angels" tells us that in all their works they are messengers "*angeloi*" of the One God, who created them as well as ourselves.

And call to mind the way that people in ancient times worshipped the gods. This invariably took the form of *sacrifice*, usually of animals, and the gods received the animal sacrifices as a necessary form of nourishment.

In today's Gospel, Christ reverses this arrangement, and shows that he is a different sort of being from the gods of the cities and the natural world. Sacrifices were made to Ceres and the gods of the land in order to ensure a bountiful harvest of wheat for bread, and to Poseidon and the gods of the rivers and streams in order to ensure the supply of fish. To Christ, no sacrifice is made, but only a prayer, and there is found bread and fish to feed 5000. Later, of course, Christ will not receive but rather *become* the sacrifice, and thereby "the bread of Life." And this is the true God, whose glory is proclaimed by the visible gods of Heaven: A source of inexhaustible life and power, needing nothing, perpetually bringing into being all that exists.

And pay close attention to the ending of this passage. The people are willing to take Jesus by force to make him become their king, but he flees into the mountains. This is in sharp contrast to the pagan kings, who were understood to be divine beings and the children of gods. In earlier times, there was no distinction between the human, political world and the spiritual world. Jesus inaugurates this distinction now, feeding the people through the overflowing life within him but rejecting temporal power.

Practice for the fourth week of Lent

Open a temple as you have been instructed. When you have done so, read the Gospel passage for this week. Enter into meditation, and visualize the scene you have just read.

See the people, gathered to hear Jesus speak on the mountain. Imagine yourself seated among them, waiting to hear the words of the Master. Then, eat with them the bread and the fish, which seems to flow without limit. Know that this is not merely physical but spiritual food, the Life that flows endlessly from the Divine.

This is Laetare Sunday, and its themes are joy, abundance, and new life. But pay attention, too, as Jesus flees into the mountains rather than be made an earthly king. This renews the theme which we saw in our reading on the First Sunday of Lent, when the Devil tempts Jesus to political power if only he will give him his worship. Consider, again, the distinction between spiritual and temporal power, and in what ways you have abandoned the former in favor of the latter.

When you have concluded your meditations, rise and offer the following prayer:

> O Lord, thou art the source of all life and abundance.
> Nourish my soul and guide me on the paths of righteousness,
> This day and in all the seasons of my life.

In the days that follow, you may take the themes for your meditation from the Gospel, the relevant passage from Genesis, or the discussion of the themes of this week.

Meditation upon the Rose

As noted above, on Rose Sunday a special golden rose is blessed by the Pope as a symbol of the joy of this season. The rose is an important symbol, as we have noted, an image of the heart, of joy, and of divine love. The following meditation on the golden rose will help you connect with that symbolism. It also works as a subtle but potent method of energetic healing, both for yourself and others.

Preparation. No special preparation is necessary. This work can be performed as a meditation in any setting, but if you wish to open a magical temple, an image of a rose (preferably golden) or an actual rose on the altar is appropriate, and you may wish to burn rose-scented incense.

Step 1. Open a magical temple, or perform the Banishing Sign of the Cross.

Step 2. Say the words:

> O God, by Whose word and power all things have been created, by Whose will all things are directed, I humbly ask that thou wilt pour forth into my heart thy light and thy truth this day, that the golden rose of joy and divine may take root therein and blossom.

Step 3. Take your seat, and calm your body with rhythmic breathing.

Slowly bring your attention to your heart center. Become aware of your heart as a center of life, vitality, and emotion. Feel and know that this life comes from God, to whom you are always connected.

Step 4. Imagine golden sunlight descending in a column from Heaven and pouring into your heart. The sunlight fills your heart with joy, healing, and awareness of divine love, and it forms itself into the shape of a golden rose, with your heart at the center. The rose drinks in the sunlight of divine joy and love, which continues to radiate from Heaven, and begins to radiate that light outward. Feel it expand throughout your body, bringing divine love, joy and healing to the column of energy that runs through the center line of your body; to your internal organs; radiating outward through your bones, muscles, and the surface of your skin. Continue from there, and feel the light radiate outward into the sphere of vital energies that surrounds your physical body.

From there, you may continue, and imagine the light radiating outward from you, filling your physical surroundings, and then expanding outward to your family, your friends, the people you see on your morning commute, people you work with, even people who don't like you, even plants and animals, even natural landscapes, inanimate objects, buildings, neighborhoods, or cities where you spend time.

If there is anyone—or anything—toward which you'd like to extend a particular blessing, you can spend some extra time concentrating on their image, imagining the golden light filling them with blessing, healing, divine love and joy. Silently pray that they may know blessing and healing through the Life that is forever in Almighty God.

Step 5. Slowly draw your attention back inward, to yourself, to the rose at your heart. Then release the visualization, but be aware that the rose, the life within you which comes from God Himself, remains always.

Step 6. Rise, and offer the following prayer.

> In the sign of the Golden Rose, oh Lord, we exult in Thy name and manifest our joy. Through this sign I pray that thou wilt confer upon us true and perfect healing of body and soul and joy in the knowledge of Thy love and our salvation. Do thou remit sin, strengthen faith, increase piety, protect us in Thy mercy, drive away all things adverse to us, and make us safe and prosperous. May all thy children be united in joy, in thy healing light and thy eternal love, and remain happy without end in eternal glory together with all the saints. Amen.

Step 7. Close your temple as instructed.

The Golden Rose meditation may be repeated at any time and may even be used as a form of daily meditation.

Passion Sunday and Passiontide

> *Hodie, si vocem Domini audieritis, nolite obdurare corda vestrum.*
> Today, if you hear the Voice of the Lord, harden not your hearts.

The Fifth Sunday of Lent is called Passion Sunday. This is, historically, an important feast of the Church, though now suppressed, like many such feasts, by the wise men of the 1960s.

The Introit to today's Mass comes from Psalm 42:

> *Judica me, Deus, et discerne causam meam de gente non sancta: ab homine iniquo et doloso erue me.*

> Judge me, O God, and discern my cause from an unholy people. From the deceitful and impious man deliver me.

Passion Sunday inaugurates a season called Passiontide, which includes both this week and Holy Week, which follows it. As Gesimatide acts as a kind of pre-Lent, in which we prepare for the Lenten Fast, Passiontide is itself a deeper Lent, for which the earlier part of the season has been a preparation. During this time, we must double down on our works of prayer, of repentance, and of almsgiving, and we must strive to maintain and even deepen our fast.

In order to understand Passiontide, we need to first do a bit of etymological work. The meaning of the word "passion" has shifted over time, and we need to understand it as our ancestors understood it if we are to experience it as they did.

Way back in 2003, I was riding on a city bus and overheard a conversation in which a woman was talking about going to see what was then a new movie, Mel Gibson's *The Passion of the Christ*. Listening to the woman talk, it was clear that she thought that the title was "Christ's Passions," and that it referred to something that Jesus had felt very strongly about. That's the usual meaning of the word "passion" or "passionate" in modern culture: a strong feeling or motivating desire. Young people at job interviews are taught to say things like, "I have a passion for great customer service." Hobbyists will talk about their "passion" for bird watching or beer brewing. And if Christ had a passion, it must have been something he thought was awfully important.

In these concepts, there is an echo, but an echo only, of the real meaning of the word. In Latin, passion or *passio* means *suffering*. Christ's passion is his suffering at the hands of Caiaphas, Pilate, and the Roman soldiers, his suffering as he carried his cross, his suffering on the cross itself.

And yet, even this doesn't truly arrive at the meaning of the word. Passion doesn't *just* mean "suffering" in the usual sense of experiencing something painful. The word passion is related to the word *passive*. Here, again, the shifting nature of language will mislead us. In our usual way of speaking, *passive* simply means "doing nothing." A person who sits around watching TV all day is described as "passive." A person who doesn't stand up for themselves is told to "stop being so passive." I recently heard a therapist talk about how often she sees couples in which the wives wish their husbands wouldn't be "so passive," and it was clear that by "passive" she simply meant "lazy."

Christ was passive to the acts of Caiaphas and Pilate, and the Roman soldiers. That does not mean he was being lazy.

So what does it mean?

The two forces

There are two forces in the Universe, two powers which emerge into being after the unimaginable unity of the First Beginning. In the tradition of the Cabala, these are called Chokhma and Binah. In the Taoist tradition of China, they are called Yang and Yin. One of these, the power which the Cabalists call "Chokhma" and the Taoists call "Yang," is the active force. The other, which the Cabalists call "Binah" and the Taoists call "Yin" is the passive force. The active force is the power of acting upon other things. The passive force is the power of *being acted upon*.

Neither is good nor evil. Both are necessary for existence. And both are present in all things and in all activities. A farmer, planting a seed, is active, or yang; the soil, receiving and nurturing the seed, is passive, or yin. Both are necessary if there is to be a harvest. And note well that, at harvest time, it is the land, which gives the fruit, which is yang; the farmer, who receives the fruit, who is yin. Thus, the two forces interpenetrate one another, create one another, and complete one another.

The two forces are often understood as masculine and feminine, but this can be misleading. To host a party and invite guests is yin, feminine, passive; to attend the party as a guest is yang, masculine, active. A man who hosts a party is passive to his guests, and in fact hopes to be as passive as possible, so that many guests may come and enjoy themselves. A woman who attends the party is active; she goes forth from her place and brings something with her, which changes the situation in which she finds herself. The man, seeing the woman at his party, approaches her to begin a conversation: Now he becomes active; if she is open to the conversation, she makes herself passive. (What happens afterward is their own business.)

We might think of certain activities as active or masculine, and others as passive or feminine, but even this is an illusion. To throw a punch is active; to block a punch is passive; a boxer who can only do one thing or the other will lose the fight. Both forces must be present, in all things, and in the appropriate form. A student must be passive to his teacher if he wishes to learn anything at all; a teacher who is passive to her students will lose control of her classroom. And yet, the student must be active in questioning his teacher and in turning in his assignments; the teacher must be passive in listening to her students and learning from them in turn.

This may seem very abstract, but it is not. To understand the power of the passive is to understand the full power and meaning of Christ.

The philosophers of the pagan world into which Christ was born were quite aware of these concepts—indeed, the Cabala itself, which treats of this subject in detail, is rooted in the philosophical traditions of the pagan Platonists and Pythagoreans. And yet it was precisely Christ's passion, His *passivity*, which kept the pagans and the Jews of the ancient world from understanding Him. As Saint Paul wrote, "We preach Christ crucified, unto the Jews a stumbling block, and unto the Greeks foolishness."

Among the pagan philosophers, it was the doctrine that God could *never be passive*. That is, to be a God was to be *unable to be acted upon*. There is a certain truth to this. The wise know that by our prayers we do not change God's mind about anything, but act instead to change ourselves—or, rather, to open ourselves to his power to change us. To pray is to become passive to God.

And yet ...

By rendering God, or the various gods, incapable of passivity, the pagans also stripped them of their total power. Even so wise a philosopher as Porphyry of Tyre rejected Christ for this very reason: *He suffered.* It never seems to have occurred to Porphyry that a God who can never be acted upon is a limited God. It is precisely in his suffering and in his passion that we see that Christ is, indeed, the complete Logos, the true and living image of the Divine Mind and the Divine Mind itself. To be truly God is and must be to contain all things: The active and the passive, the masculine and the feminine, the Heavens and the Earth. Christ's providence and his very existence extends from the beginning of things in the unknowable Godhead down to the very last of things, when he descends into Hell after His Death on the Cross. And then it returns again, from the last of things in Hell, back to the beginning of things, at the right hand of the Father.

The aim of the spiritual life is to become divinized, to become like unto God Himself, as far as this is possible.

And what this means is that we ourselves must embrace both powers, the active and the passive. We must be capable of action and capable of being acted upon. We must be passive even when this means truly suffering, as it often does: "Take up your cross and follow me."

Genesis

> And God said, Let the waters bring forth abundantly the moving creature that hath life, and fowl that may fly above the earth in the open firmament of heaven. And God created great whales, and every living creature that moveth, which the waters brought forth abundantly, after their kind, and every winged fowl after his kind: and God saw that it was good. And God blessed them, saying, Be fruitful, and multiply, and fill the waters in the seas, and let fowl multiply in the earth.

Recall what we said last week about the activity of the Sun and Moon, and the stars: They are for times and seasons. In the Creation myth, we now have the emergence of living beings who move under their own power. This is the work of the *vital soul*, which, in esoteric symbolism, is closely linked to the Sun.

The Gospel

At that time, Jesus said to the crowds of the Jews, "Which of you shall convince me of sin? If I say the truth to you, why do you not believe me: He that is of God heareth the words of God. Therefore you hear them not, because you are not of God."

The Jews therefore answered and said to him: "Do not we say well that thou art a Samaritan and hast a devil?" Jesus answered: "I have not a devil: but I honour my Father. And you have dishonoured me. But I seek not my own glory: there is one that seeketh and judgeth. Amen, amen, I say to you: If any man keep my word, he shall not see death for ever."

The Jews therefore said: "Now we know that thou hast a devil. Abraham is dead, and the prophets: and thou sayest: If any man keep my word, he shall not taste death for ever. Art thou greater than our father Abraham, who is dead? And the prophets are dead. Whom dost thou make thyself?"

Jesus answered: "If I glorify myself, my glory is nothing. It is my Father that glorifieth me, of whom you say that he is your God. And you have not known him: but I know him. And if I shall say that I know him not, I shall be like to you, a liar. But I do know him and do keep his word. Abraham your father rejoiced that he might see my day: he saw it and was glad." The Jews therefore said to him: "Thou art not yet fifty years old. And hast thou seen Abraham?" Jesus said to them: "Amen, amen, I say to you, before Abraham was made, I AM." They took up stones therefore to cast at him. But Jesus hid himself and went out of the temple.

Themes of Passion Sunday

Today is Passion Sunday, and this week, therefore, begins the true commemoration of Christ's Passion: His suffering and death on the Cross. Our Gospel reading today, therefore, is deeply concerned with Death and its Mysteries.

> If any man keep my word, he shall not see Death forever.

Thus Christ teaches his people, but they are unwilling to hear him. Abraham and the prophets are dead, they say. We know that, at this time, there were some among the Jewish people who believed in the Resurrection of the dead, and others who did not. We know which sort of Jesus is faced with today. The historical detail, however, is truly unimportant. What is important is that these people *believe in the dominion of Death*. They are, therefore, under the power of Death, and the World of the Dead.

Remember what we have said. Sin and Death are not mere concepts or unconscious forces. They are powers within this world of ours, Heaven's basement and Hell's rooftop garden.

> Before Abraham was, I AM.

A great deal of information lies hidden in this simple sentence.

I AM is the great Name of God, given to Moses in the speech of the Burning Bush: I AM. In Hebrew, AHIA, Eh-hei-yeh. In this simple phrase, God identifies himself with existence, the very source of being. And being comes before non-being.

Abraham is dead, they say, and the prophets are dead. But we have already learned that this is not true; we have already seen Christ glorified, transfigured, in the company of Moses and Elijah. The prophets are not dead but have transcended the realm of Death.

How is this done?

> If any man keep my word, he shall not see death for ever.
> It is my Father that glorifieth me.
> I AM.

In the tradition of the Cabala, this I AM is the highest Name of God, the Name of Kether, the very ground of being itself. The Jews in the temple, who believe that Abraham is dead, who throw rocks at the living Messiah: These are all people under the dominion of Death. They believe in Death and, thus, are faithful to Death. But God is prior to Death; before Abraham was, I AM. By uniting ourself to God the Father, becoming like unto God, we transcend the world of Death, and the power of Death. And Death shall have no more dominion.

And how are we to do this? We continue on our Lenten pilgrimage, and arrive soon at Easter. The time is coming when all shall be revealed.

Practice for the fifth week of Lent

Open a temple as you have been instructed. When you have done so, read the Gospel passage for this week. Enter into meditation, and visualize the scene you have just read. See the crowd, once again accusing Jesus of being a demoniac, and listen as he rebukes them.

Consider seriously those words, "If I glorify myself, my glory is nothing. It is my Father that glorifieth me, of whom you say that he is your God." And consider that ancient Name of God: "I AM." Imagine God, the source of all being, as the Sun, and imagine your own soul like a planet orbiting that Sun and illuminated by its light. Like the surface of the Earth, the soul cannot produce its own light, but receives the light of the Sun and becomes visible. This, again, is the True Self, the Divine Will made manifest. Everything else is darkness and accretion.

When you conclude your meditations, rise, and offer the following prayer:

> May all glory be unto thee Oh Lord.
> Oh thou who hast brought forth all life upon the Earth,
> And may all thy creations be glorified in thy holy light.

In the days that follow, you may take the themes for your meditation from the Gospel, the relevant passage from Genesis, or the discussion of the themes of this week.

The Friday of Sorrows

The Friday of Passion Week is called the Friday of Sorrows, and it is dedicated to the Seven Sorrows of Mary. There is another feast dedicated to Our Lady of Sorrows in September, and the modern Church has suppressed the Friday of Sorrows in its favor. That's no reason, however, why we can't carry on the devotion to the Seven Sorrows of Mary in our private work. Recall what we said at the beginning of this book about the value of holy sorrow, as well as holy joy.

There is a chaplet similar to the Rosary dedicated to the Seven Sorrows of Mary, and today is a good day to make use of it. If you don't have a physical chaplet, don't worry; you can pray the chaplet prayers without a physical guide if necessary. All you really need is the ability to count to seven.

Seven Sorrows meditation

Step 1. You may begin by opening a magical temple, or simply perform the Banishing Sign of the Cross.

Step 2. Say the following prayer, from the traditional Collect for today's Mass:

> O God, in whose Passion, according to the prophecy of Simeon, the sword of sorrow didst pierce the most sweet soul of the glorious Mary, Virgin and Mother; mercifully grant that we who call to mind with veneration her anguish and suffering, by the glorious merits and prayers of all the Saints who faithfully stood beneath the Cross interceding for us, may obtain the blessed fruit of Thy Passion, Thou Who livest and reigneth with God the Father, in the unity of the Holy Ghost, one God, world without end. Amen.

Step 3. Pray the Seven Sorrows chaplet. This is done in the following way.

First, say the Our Father, three Hail Marys, and the Glory Be.

Second, announce the first Sorrow—or the second, third, and so on. The sorrows, in order, are as follows:

1. The prophecy of Simeon, that a sword would pierce the heart of Mary
2. The flight into Egypt, when the Holy Family is forced to flee from King Herod
3. The loss of the child Jesus for three days
4. Mary's encounter with Jesus as he carries his cross
5. Mary at the foot of the cross while Jesus is crucified
6. Mary receiving the body of Jesus
7. The body of Jesus is placed in the tomb.

For each Sorrow, pray:

> One our Father
> Seven Hail Marys
> Holy Mother hear my prayers, and renew in my heart each wound of Jesus my Savior.

The usual instructions for devotions of this sort suggest that you meditate on each Sorrow *while* praying the Hail Marys. I personally find it difficult to do both things at the same time, and impossible if I'm praying silently, as I would in a public place. I therefore find it more helpful to meditate for a short time immediately after announcing the Sorrow, visualizing or contemplating the scene described, and then releasing the meditation and saying the prayers as a kind of mantra. You may find that method helpful as well.

After the Seventh Sorrow, say the following prayer.

> Let intercession be made for us, we beseech Thee, O Lord Jesus Christ, now and at the hour of our death, before the throne of Thy mercy, by the Most Blessed Virgin Mary, Thy Mother, whose most holy soul was pierced by a sword of sorrow in the hour of Thy Passion. Through Thee, O Christ, savior of the world, Who with the Father and the Holy Spirit lives and reigns world without end. Amen.
>
> Mary, who was conceived without sin and who suffered for us, pray for us.
>
> Mary, who was conceived without sin and who suffered for us, pray for us.
>
> Mary, who was conceived without sin and who suffered for us, pray for us.

Close with the Sign of the Cross, or the usual closing if you are working in an open temple.

Palm Sunday and Holy Week

Today is Palm Sunday, and the beginning of Holy Week. This is the day of Christ's entry in triumph into Jerusalem.

The Introit today reads:

> *Domine, ne longe facias auxilium tuum a me, ad defensionem meam aspice: libera me de ore leonis, et a cornibus unicornium humilitatem meam.*
>
> O Lord, be not far from me with Thy aid; hasten to assist me. Save me from the lion's mouth, and preserve my wretched life from the horns of the unicorns.

Genesis

On the Sixth Day, Mankind comes into existence:

> And God said, Let us make man in our image, after our likeness: and let them have dominion over the fish of the sea, and over the fowl of the air, and over the cattle, and over all the earth, and over every creeping thing that creepeth upon the earth.
>
> So God created man in his own image, in the image of God created He him; male and female created He them.
>
> And God blessed them, and God said unto them, Be fruitful, and multiply, and replenish the earth, and subdue it: and have dominion over the fish of the sea, and over the fowl of the air, and over every living thing that moveth upon the earth.
>
> And God said, Behold, I have given you every herb bearing seed, which is upon the face of all the earth, and every tree, in the which is the fruit of a tree yielding seed; to you it shall be for meat.
>
> And to every beast of the earth, and to every fowl of the air, and to every thing that creepeth upon the earth, wherein there is life, I have given every green herb for meat: and it was so.
>
> And God saw every thing that he had made, and, behold, it was very good. And the evening and the morning were the Sixth Day.

As we shall see, there are two Gospel readings for today. The first is read during the blessing of the palms or other branches; the second is read during the Mass itself. The first concerns Christ's entry into Jerusalem in triumph. The second is the Passion narrative as given by Matthew.

As we read the Passion narrative today, we have truly entered into the time and into the Mystery of the Passion and death of Our Lord, Jesus Christ, the New Adam. Today, therefore, marks the completion of the Mystery of the Sixth Day. Man has come into being; but God has not yet come to rest from His work.

The blessing of palms

The best-known tradition associated with Palm Sunday is, of course, the blessing of palms. In many a Catholic household, one can see palm branches, distributed during today's Mass, twined behind the crucifix. The palm branches commemorate the branches which were laid before Our Lord by the crowd.

Now, this custom originated in the Middle East, where palm or olive branches are widely available. As it spread to the Northern parts of the world, it became common to use local trees. In this age of global trade networks, palm branches are widely used, but we should consider the opportunity provided by the older custom. The palm branches, once consecrated, become magical talismans which are able to ward off evil spirits and devices of hostile magicians. At one time, it was common to burn the consecrated palm fronds in order to ward off hostile magic, and in fact this use was widespread enough that the Modernist church felt the need to condemn it; we may therefore be assured of its usefulness. Many trees have natural magical properties which can strengthen the protective effect of the blessing, and some are far better than the palm. Most evergreens are good. Cedar and juniper in particular have been used throughout the world to clear negative energy and repel hostile magic; I strongly recommend them.

A ceremony for the blessing of branches

By this point in our journey, you know how this goes. Set up your altar in the usual way, and place the branches you intend to consecrate upon it. Then read the following passage, from the Gospel of Matthew:

> At that time, And when they drew nigh to Jerusalem and were come to Bethphage, unto mount Olivet, then Jesus sent two disciples, saying to them: "Go ye into the village that is over against you: and immediately you shall find an ass tied and a colt with her. Loose them and bring them to me. And if any man shall say anything to you, say ye that the Lord hath need of them. And forthwith he will let them go."
>
> Now, all this was done that it might be fulfilled which was spoken by the prophet, saying: "Tell ye the daughter of Sion: 'Behold thy king cometh to thee, meek and sitting upon an ass and a colt, the foal of her that is used to the yoke.'"
>
> And the disciples, going, did as Jesus commanded them. And they brought the ass and the colt and laid their garments upon them and made him sit thereon. And a very great multitude spread their garments in the way: and others cut boughs from the trees and strewed them in the way.
>
> And the multitudes that went before and that followed cried, saying: "Hosanna to the son of David: Blessed is he that cometh in the name of the Lord: Hosanna in the highest."

After the usual preparatory work, call down the energy of the Holy Spirit, and say the following words of consecration over the branches:

> O Lord, bless + these branches of palm [or whatever tree you've chosen]. Grant that the sincere devotion of Your people may make them victorious over their enemy and zealous in works of mercy, and thus spiritually complete the ceremony which they outwardly perform this day in Your honor. Through Christ our Lord, Amen.

They are now a consecrated Sacramental, and you may use them for whatever purpose you like. Traditionally, they are interlaced behind the corpus on your home crucifix, and they may be burned throughout the year for purposes of spiritual protection and energetic purification.

The Gospel

In earlier times, the ceremony of the blessing and distribution of palms took place before the Mass, and had (as we've seen above) its own Gospel. The Gospel reading for the Mass itself was Matthew 26:1–75 and Matthew 27:1–66—that is, the entire Passion narrative according to Saint Matthew.

This sets the stage for the week to come. We are, magically speaking, already acting within the Passion, and the presence of the Passion will increase in intensity as we approach Good Friday, when it will finally reach its culmination.

It would be ideal to perform two meditations today: in the first, perform the blessing of palms (or other branches), and in the second, a reading and meditation upon the Passion narrative in an open temple. For many people, a single period of ritual or meditation is as much as they have time for. In this case, you may either fold the two into one ceremony, by continuing into the passion narrative after the blessing of the palms, or else pick one of the two.

The prayer for Palm Sunday comes from the Gospel narrative:

> Hosanna to the son of David: Blessed is he that cometh in the name of the Lord: Hosanna in the highest.

CHAPTER FIVE

The Easter Triduum

Holy Week practice
Meditations for the first three days of Holy Week

The Monday, Tuesday, and Wednesday of Holy Week are days of preparation. During your meditations on these days, you may read and meditate on the Gospels traditionally associated with them. These are:

> Monday. John 12:1–9. This recounts the anointing of the feet of Jesus by Martha.
> Tuesday. Mark 14:1–72 and 15:1–46. This is the Passion narrative according to Saint Mark.
> Wednesday. Luke 22:1–71 and Luke 23:1–53. This is the Passion narrative according to Saint Luke.

Additional practices of Holy Week

Holy Week is a very common time to receive the sacrament of Confession. It was common during the Middle Ages for people to receive Communion once a year, at Easter, and this was preceded by Confession. In your own work, you may wish to practice the Confiteor Ritual at this time.

Holy Week has also, interestingly, been a traditional time for Spring cleaning. This is a physical act which reflects a spiritual process. Just as, through fasting and repentance, we purify our souls, so too we may purify our homes and physical spaces.

Wednesday of Holy Week is known as Spy Wednesday, as this is said to be the day of the treachery of Judas, the spy. Many churches hold Tenebrae services on this day. Tenebrae means "darkness," and the service involves chanting the Matins and Lauds of Maundy Thursday, while a set of candles is extinguished one by one. You might consider attending a public chanting of the Tenebrae if a church near you makes it available.

Maundy Thursday

The name of Maundy Thursday comes from the Latin word "mandatum," that is, "commandment." This refers to the new commandment, given by Jesus to the disciples at the Last Supper:

> A new commandment I give unto you, That ye love one another; as I have loved you, that ye also love one another. By this shall all men know that ye are my disciples, if ye have love one to another.

The ritual focus of the Western Church on Maundy Thursday is the washing of the feet. In some countries, it was common for the king or queen to wash the feet of the poor, in remembrance of the washing of the feet of the Disciples by Christ after the Last Supper. The washing of the feet is celebrated to this day in many churches. It may be performed by the priest or by the faithful for one another.

It's worth considering what "foot washing" means in a symbolic sense. The foot is the part of the body which touches the ground and moves us about in this world, and is thus a symbol for our contact with the world of matter. In that sense, the foot is a representation of the body as a whole, because it is through the body and its senses that we interact with the material world. In the washing of His disciples' feet, Jesus purifies the material body of the Disciples, removing the accretions of matter and allowing them to act in the material world without being drawn down by it.

Bells are rung this day, and then silenced, and will not be heard again until Easter. In many countries in earlier times, children would run through the street announcing the time for Mass, in lieu of bells;

the bells themselves had, it was said, gone to Rome to be absolved of their sins. Of course, this often led to Trick-or-Treating, sending children door to door to ask for candy, having been the usual way our forebears had for celebrating holidays of any kind.

At the close of the Mass on Maundy Thursday, the altars are stripped, the host removed to an altar of repose, as no hosts are consecrated during the liturgies on Good Friday and Holy Saturday. During this time, the 21st Psalm (or 22nd, in Protestant Bibles) is sung:

> O God my God, look upon me: why hast thou forsaken me? Far from my salvation are the words of my sins.
> O my God, I shall cry by day, and thou wilt not hear: and by night, and it shall not be reputed as folly in me.
> But thou dwellest in the holy place, the praise of Israel.
> In thee have our fathers hoped: they have hoped, and thou hast delivered them.
> They cried to thee, and they were saved: they trusted in thee, and were not confounded.
> But I am a worm, and no man: the reproach of men, and the outcast of the people.
> All they that saw me have laughed me to scorn: they have spoken with the lips, and wagged the head.
> "He hoped in the Lord, let him deliver him: let him save him, seeing he delighteth in him."
> For thou art he that hast drawn me out of the womb: my hope from the breasts of my mother.
> I was cast upon thee from the womb. From my mother's womb thou art my God,
> Depart not from me. For tribulation is very near: for there is none to help me.
> Many calves have surrounded me: fat bulls have besieged me.
> They have opened their mouths against me, as a lion ravening and roaring.
> I am poured out like water; and all my bones are scattered. My heart is become like wax melting in the midst of my bowels. My strength is dried up like a potsherd, and my tongue hath cleaved to my jaws: and thou hast brought me down into the dust of death.
> For many dogs have encompassed me: the council of the malignant hath besieged me. They have dug my hands and feet.

> They have numbered all my bones. And they have looked and stared upon me.
> They parted my garments amongst them; and upon my vesture they cast lots.
> But thou, O Lord, remove not thy help to a distance from me; look towards my defense.
> Deliver, O God, my soul from the sword: my only one from the hand of the dog.
> Save me from the lion's mouth; and my lowness from the horns of the unicorns.
> I will declare thy name to my brethren: in the midst of the church will I praise thee.
> Ye that fear the Lord, praise him: all ye the seed of Jacob, glorify him.
> Let all the seed of Israel fear him: because he hath not slighted nor despised the supplication of the poor man. Neither hath he turned away his face form me: and when I cried to him he heard me.
> With thee is my praise in a great church: I will pay my vows in the sight of them that fear him.
> The poor shall eat and shall be filled: and they shall praise the Lord that seek him: their hearts shall live for ever and ever.
> All the ends of the earth shall remember, and shall be converted to the Lord: And all the kindreds of the Gentiles shall adore in his sight.
> For the kingdom is the Lord's; and he shall have dominion over the nations.
> All the fat ones of the earth have eaten and have adored: all they that go down to the earth shall fall before him.
> And to him my soul shall live: and my seed shall serve him.
> There shall be declared to the Lord a generation to come: and the heavens shall shew forth his justice to a people that shall be born, which the Lord hath made.
> They have divided my garments among them, and for my vesture they have cast lots.

The Western liturgy focuses on the washing of the feet in today's Gospel. In the Eastern Church, four moments are commemorated: the institution of the Eucharist, the washing of the feet, the agony in the garden, and the betrayal of Jesus by Judas Iscariot. In our own work, we will make use of several different elements of the day's symbolism.

The ritual of foot washing is a lovely one, but best practiced with a group. The following meditation combines the different elements of the Maundy Thursday symbolism into one, including the Gospel, a cleansing meditation, and the stripping of the altar.

Maundy Thursday meditation

Step 1. Open a temple as you have been instructed.

Step 2. Standing, with your hands in the orans posture, say:

> It is fitting that we should glory in the cross of our Lord Jesus Christ, in whom is salvation, life and resurrection for us, by whom we are saved and delivered. May God have mercy on us and bless us; may He let His face shine upon us; and may He have mercy on us.
>
> Our Lord Jesus Christ in His passion gave each one recompense according to his deserts; may He deliver us from our sins of old, and bestow on us the grace of His resurrection.

Step 3. Read today's Gospel, John 13:1–15:

> Before the festival day of the pasch, Jesus knowing that his hour was come, that he should pass out of this world to the Father: having loved his own who were in the world, he loved them unto the end. And when supper was done (the devil having now put into the heart of Judas Iscariot, the son of Simon, to betray him), Knowing that the Father had given him all things into his hands and that he came from God and goeth to God, He riseth from supper and layeth aside his garments and, having taken a towel, girded himself. After that, he putteth water into a basin and began to wash the feet of the disciples and to wipe them with the towel wherewith he was girded. He cometh therefore to Simon Peter.
>
> And Peter saith to him: "Lord, dost thou wash my feet?"
>
> Jesus answered and said to him: "What I do, thou knowest not now; but thou shalt know hereafter."
>
> Peter saith to him: "Thou shalt never wash my feet."
>
> Jesus answered him: "If I wash thee not, thou shalt have no part with me."

> Simon Peter saith to him: "Lord, not only my feet, but also my hands and my head."
> Jesus saith to him: "He that is washed needeth not but to wash his feet, but is clean wholly. And you are clean, but not all." For he knew who he was that would betray him; therefore he said: "You are not all clean."
> Then after he had washed their feet and taken his garments, being set down again, he said to them: "Know you what I have done to you? You call me Master and Lord. And you say well: for so I am. If then I being your Lord and Master, have washed your feet; you also ought to wash one another's feet. For I have given you an example, that as I have done to you, so you do also."

Step 4. Take your seat and enter into meditation as you have been instructed, calming your body and your energy with rhythmic breathing. Then visualize the scene:

Step 5. Stand with your hands in the orans posture and say the words:

> Cleans me, oh Lord, and I shall be clean; wash me, and I shall be whiter than snow.
> May I be cleansed of all sin and all darkness.

Step 6. Visualize a column of white light descending from the Heavens. Know that this is the purifying power of God. Picture it entering your body through the crown of your head and descending through you, all the way to the soles of your feet, and extending outward through your internal organs, your bones, and muscles, your skin, and expanding outward to cleanse your energetic body. This is the cleansing of the Divine Light.

Step 7. When you feel ready, take your seat. Feel the cleansing Divine Light still present with you. Gather it into your heart, the seat of the Golden Rose. Say the words:

> A new commandment I give unto you, saith the Lord: That you love one another, as I have loved you.

Step 8. As in the Golden Rose meditation, imagine the light radiating outward from your heart, bringing divine love and purification through you to your physical surroundings, your friends and family, and everyone in your life.

Step 9. When you have finished, release the image of the light. Stand with hands in the orans posture and say:

> Let these three, faith, hope, and charity, remain in you; but the greatest of these is charity. May God in his charity cause the light of His countenance to shine on us and have mercy on us always.

Step 10. Return to your seat or kneel. Close your eyes, bow your head and sit in contemplative silence.

Step 11. Rise, and say the following words:

> O God my God, look upon me: why hast thou forsaken me? Far from my salvation are the words of my sins.
>
> My enemies have surrounded me.
>
> They have opened their mouths against me, as a lion ravening and roaring.
>
> I am poured out like water; and all my bones are scattered. My heart is become like wax melting in the midst of my bowels.
>
> My strength is dried up like a potsherd, and my tongue hath cleaved to my jaws: and thou hast brought me down into the dust of death.
>
> They have divided my garments among them, and for my vesture they have cast lots.
>
> Depart not from me, Oh God. For tribulation is very near, and there is none to help me.

Step 12. Extinguish any candles or incense you may have burning. Then remove the cloth from your altar, fold it carefully, and place it next to the crucifix. Leave your space in solemn and reverent silence.

Good Friday

We now enter into the depths of the Mystery.

On Good Friday, no hosts are consecrated, nor will they be on Holy Saturday. The Good Friday liturgy is practiced in place of the usual Mass.

Good Friday is a profound and solemn time, and the traditions associated with it are accordingly serious. One of the best-known is that of the Three Holy Hours. This is the period from noon until 3:00 when Jesus is said to have hung on the cross. During this time, it is customary to take no food, and to engage in spiritual practice or meditation. This is a good time to practice the Good Friday Meditation in this chapter, and you may also wish to work with the Way of the Cross, the Rosary, or some other devotional practice.

If you like, you can turn the three hours into a kind of personal retreat in miniature in this way.

The seven last words

The tradition of the Seven Last Words has for centuries had great importance in Western spirituality, providing themes for meditation and spiritual retreats and often having been set (in their Latin translation) to music. They are not actually individual words, but rather seven phrases spoken by Jesus on the Cross. They are:

1. Luke 23:34. Father, forgive them, they know not what they do.
   Pater, dimitte illis, quia nesciunt, quid faciunt.
2. Luke 23:43. This day thou shalt be with me in Paradise.
   Hodie mecum eris in Paradiso.
3. John 19:26–27. Woman, behold thy son.
   Mulier, ecce filius tuus.
4. Mark 15:34/Matthew 27:46. My God, My God, why hast thou forsaken me?"
   Deus meus, Deus meus, utquid dereliquisti me?
   (In Aramaic) *Eli, Eli, lamma sabacthani?*
5. John 19:28. I thirst.
   Sitio.
6. John 19:30. It is finished.
   Consummatum est.
7. Luke 23:46. Into thine hands, O Lord, I commend my spirit.
   In manus tuas, Domine, commendo spíritum meum.

These words are associated with Good Friday, and, if this is your first time working with this book, you may simply wish to read and consider them today. You may also meditate on them during the Three Holy Hours. In the future—when you need something more to do—you can take each one of them as a theme for meditation during Holy Week. That is, on Palm Sunday, "Father, forgive them, they know not what they do," and so on, until you arrive at "Into thine hands, O Lord, I commend my spirit" on Holy Saturday.

The Good Friday meditation

You should wear black if you are able to.

Open a temple in the usual way. Then, standing with hands in the orans posture, say the following prayer:

Today, you should take no food at all between the hours of noon and 3:00 p.m., and avoid entertainment of any kind.

Preparation. If you have a permanent temple space, it should still be set up as it was yesterday, on Maundy Thursday. If not, make sure that you at least have a crucifix, next to which should be the purple altar cloth from yesterday's meditation.

Step 1. This is not technically a temple opening, as we did not close our temple yesterday. We will not perform the closing until Easter Sunday. Still, you should perform the Banishing Sign of the Cross, followed by the censing with incense. The asperges is not practiced this day.

Step 2. With hands in the orans posture, say the following words:

> O God who, by the Passion of Thy Christ, our Lord, hast loosened the bonds of death, that heritage of the first sin to which all men of later times did succeed: make us so conformed to Him that, as we must needs have bourne the likeness of earthly nature, so we may by sanctification bear the likeness of heavenly grace.

Step 3. Take your seat, and read the Passion narrative of St. John, that is, John 18:1–40 and 19:1–42.

Step 4. Using rhythmic breathing, enter into meditation. Visualize the entire scene which you have read, from the agony of Jesus at the garden of Gethsemane to his burial in the tomb by Joseph of Arimathea. As you do this, focus on the perspective of Jesus himself. Pray with him in the garden; with him, suffer betrayal at the hands of someone you trusted; endure condemnation and rejection. Imagine carrying the cross, and feel the nails driven into his hands and feet. Finally, allow yourself to die with him. Know that, as you do this, it is your Lower Self that dies: The bundle of passions, habits, and cultural programming that makes up the character that you play in your ordinary life.

Step 5. Rise, and offer the following prayer.

> Pour forth, I beseech Thee, O Lord, thy grace into my heart and into the hearts of all thy children. May the Way of the Cross lead me and all mankind, through the passion and death of thine only Son, to the Glory of His Resurrection. Amen.

Step 6. Extinguish the candles on your altar and any incense still burning. Then, unfold the altar cloth, and use it to wrap the crucifix. Lay the folded crucifix on the altar and leave your space in solemn and reverent silence. If you have performed the meditation during the Three Holy Hours, you may continue with whatever other practices you have in mind.

Holy Saturday: The Harrowing of Hell

Easter Water

On Holy Saturday, a special type of holy water called Easter Water is prepared. In *The Book of Sacramental Magic*, I provided a ritual for making holy water at home. This is very similar, but there are a few differences.

The esoteric meaning of the Harrowing of Hell

This is one of the secrets of the esoteric tradition. As always, you're free to accept it or to reject it. We are, in a certain, real sense, already in the World of the Dead.

It isn't the lowest or the worst part. In the *Iliad*, Homer speaks of the realm of Tartarus into which the titans and the giants, the enemies of the gods, have been cast. Tartarus, he says, is as far below the Underworld of the human Dead as that realm is below the Heaven of the Gods. In our tradition, that is Hell or Gehenna, the deep pit into which Satan and his apostate angels—the Christian equivalent to the titans and the giants—have been cast. Above this is Hades, the Realm of the Dead.

And this Earth on which we walk and live our lives?

The ancients and the medievals, as you know, saw the Earth as the center of the universe and believed that the planets, the Moon, and the Sun revolved around it. This isn't a very useful cosmology, if your goal is to send robots to Mars or to take pictures of distant planets.

As a map of the spiritual world and a guide to human psychology, however, it fails in comparison with the ancient view. Many modern people believe that, because our ancestors saw the Earth as the center of the cosmos, they must have thought it was the most important place in the cosmos. This is not true. The Earth was the center, but it was also thought of as the *bottom*.

Go outside at night and look up at the Heavens. What you will see, if you forget your modern training in astronomy, is a collection of brilliant and orderly lights. To our ancestors, these were the visible Heavens. In the planets and the stars, they saw living, divine beings, the bodies, or at least, the images, of gods or angels. The Christian Scriptures share this view. The Sun, the Moon, and the stars, as we have seen, are given to us for times and seasons. The "Heavens proclaim the glory of God," and "There is nowhere their voice is not heard." At Christmas, the Magi follow the guidance of a star to find the infant Jesus—and in recent years, that star has been plausibly identified as a conjunction of Jupiter, planet of the king of the Gods, and Regulus, the star which represents kingship, in the sign of Leo, the lion and symbol of the tribe of Judah. This took place in the year 3 B.C., and that year is therefore a probable date for the birth of Christ.

Our world, on the other hand, is a world of change and mixture—a world of chaos. Moreover, our condition here is one in which our souls seem to be imprisoned within our bodies. What are bodies? Material creations, Earth; without our souls to animate them, they are dead. We are, therefore, effectively imprisoned within death. As Plato wrote, *Soma is sema*, "The body is a tomb."

Again, the Christian Scriptures and the apocrypha share or seem to share this worldview. Who is it that is called "The Prince of This World?" None other than Satan, the Lord of the Dead.

And so we are, in a sense, already in Hades.

Again, not in the worst part. We are also alive and ensouled. We are also in a place in which we can encounter the angels and the saints, and in which we can, in the Sacraments, encounter the Living God who is the font of all life. This is Hades, but it isn't *just* Hades. In another sense, we're also already in Heaven. "The Kingdom of God is among you." I think of the Earth as Hell's rooftop garden: A nice place, but you want to avoid the downstairs neighbors.

The point, for our purposes, is this: The Harrowing of Hell is an event in time, perhaps, but, more importantly, an event in mythic time: It always *is*. The Hades from which the souls of the Dead are released is not just the Underworld. It is *our world*. The condition of Hades is not just the condition of the Afterlife for those born in time before Christ. It is the condition in which we are all trapped: The cycle of birth and death, incarnation and reincarnation. It is this cycle which is broken for all time by the work of Christ on the Cross: "This day you will be with me in Paradise."

Now, because this takes place outside of time, it must be the case that the way out has always, to a certain extent, been broken: At least to those who can find the way. This was fewer, perhaps, before the incarnation; and it is rarer, we are taught, for those who work outside the Christian tradition. But we know that it was known in earlier times. In the dialogues *Phaedo* and *Phaedrus*, Plato described the true Heaven as beyond the spheres of the visible Heavens, and the way out as available to those who followed his discipline of philosophy. In the sacred writings of India, too, we find an understanding of the means of escape from incarnation and return to the Divine: This is the whole point both of the Vedantic and the Buddhist traditions. And, of course, we learn in our own Scriptures—including the story we have just read—that some among the prophets ascended to Heaven rather than into the Underworld.

The Holy Saturday meditation

The following meditation should, if possible, be practiced in the evening, preferably after the sun has set.

Step 1. Return to your temple space, or set it up again. On the altar should be a single candle, unlit, the crucifix still wrapped in purple cloth. Perform the Banishing Sign of the Cross and the censing with incense.

Step 2. Stand with your hands in the orans posture, and say the words:

> Today is Holy Saturday. Today, our Lord Jesus descends into the place of the Dead to liberate all those who have gone before us from the captivity of Satan and Death.
>
> The Lord is my portion, said my soul: therefore will I wait for him.
>
> The Lord is good to them that hope in him, to the soul that seeketh Him.

It is good to wait with silence for the salvation of God.

Jerusalem, Jerusalem, be converted to the Lord thy God.

He was led like a sheep to the slaughter, and whilst he was ill-used, he opened not his mouth: he was delivered over to death: that he might give life to his people. He delivered himself up to death, and was reckoned among the wicked.

O Lord Jesus Christ, the Resurrection and the life of the world, grant us grace that we may give an account of Thy resurrection, and Thy miracles which Thou didst in Hades.

Step 3. Take your seat, and read the following selection from *The Gospel of Nicodemus*:

And Seth said: Prophets and patriarchs, hear. When my father Adam, the first created, was about to fall once upon a time into death, he sent me to make entreaty to God very close by the gate of paradise, that He would guide me by an angel to the tree of compassion and that I might take oil and anoint my father, and that he might rise up from his sickness: which thing, therefore, I also did. And after the prayer an angel of the Lord came, and said to me: What, Seth, dost thou ask? Dost thou ask oil which raiseth up the sick, or the tree from which this oil flows, on account of the sickness of thy father? This is not to be found now. Go, therefore, and tell thy father, that after the accomplishing of 5500 years from the creation of the world, thou shall come into the earth the only-begotten Son of God, being made man; and He shall anoint him with this oil, and shall raise him up; and shall wash clean, with water and with the Holy Spirit, both him and those out of him, and then shall he be healed of every disease; but now this is impossible.

When the patriarchs and the prophets heard these words, they rejoiced greatly.

And when all were in such joy, came Satan the heir of darkness, and said to Hades: O all-devouring and insatiable, hear my words. There is of the race of the Jews one named Jesus, calling himself the Son of God; and being a man, by our working with them the Jews have crucified him: and now when he is dead, be ready that we may secure him here. For I know that he is a man, and I heard him also saying, My soul is exceeding sorrowful, even unto death. He has also done me many evils when living with mortals in the upper world. For wherever he found my servants, he persecuted them; and whatever men I made crooked, blind, lame, lepers, or any such thing, by a single word he healed them; and many whom I had got ready to be buried, even these through a single word he brought to life again.

Hades says: And is this man so powerful as to do such things by a single word? or if he be so, canst thou withstand him? It seems to me that, if he be so, no one will be able to withstand him. And if thou sayest that thou didst hear him dreading death, he said this mocking thee, and laughing, wishing to seize thee with the strong hand; and woe, woe to thee, to all eternity!

Satan says: O all-devouring and insatiable Hades, art thou so afraid at hearing of our common enemy? I was not afraid of him, but worked in the Jews, and they crucified him, and gave him also to drink gall with vinegar. Make ready, then, in order that you may lay fast hold of him when he comes.

Hades answered: Heir of darkness, son of destruction, devil, thou hast just now told me that many whom thou hadst made ready to be buried, be brought to life again by a single word. And if he has delivered others from the tomb, how and with what power shall he be laid hold of by us? For I not long ago swallowed down one dead, Lazarus by name; and not long after, one of the living by a single word dragged him up by force out of my bowels: and I think that it was he of whom thou speakest. If, therefore, we receive him here, I am afraid lest perchance we be in danger even about the rest. For, lo, all those that I have swallowed from eternity I perceive to be in commotion, and I am pained in my belly. And the snatching away of Lazarus beforehand seems to me to be no good sign: for not like a dead body, but like an eagle, he flew out of me; for so suddenly did the earth throw him out. Wherefore also I adjure even thee, for thy benefit and for mine, not to bring him here; for I think that he is coming here to raise all the dead. And this I tell thee: by the darkness in which we live, if thou bring him here, not one of the dead will be left behind in it to me.

While Satan and Hades were thus speaking to each other, there was a great voice like thunder, saying: Lift up your gates, O ye rulers; and be ye lifted up, ye everlasting gates; and the King of glory shall come in. When Hades heard, he said to Satan: Go forth, if thou art able, and withstand him. Satan therefore went forth to the outside. Then Hades says to his demons: Secure well and strongly the gates of brass and the bars of iron, and attend to my bolts, and stand in order, and see to everything; for if he come in here, woe will seize us.

The forefathers having heard this, began all to revile him, saying: O all-devouring and insatiable! open, that the King of glory may come in. David the prophet says: Dost thou not know, O blind, that I when living in the world prophesied this saying: Lift up your gates, O ye rulers? Hesaias said: I, foreseeing this by the Holy Spirit, wrote: The dead shall rise up, and those in their tombs shall be raised, and those in the earth shall rejoice. And where, O death, is thy sting? where, O Hades, is thy victory?

There came, then, again a voice saying: Lift up the gates. Hades, hearing the voice the second time, answered as if forsooth he did not know, and says: Who is this King of glory? The angels of the Lord say: The Lord strong and mighty, the Lord mighty in battle. And immediately with these words the brazen gates were shattered, and the iron bars broken, and all the dead who had been bound came out of the prisons, and we with them. And the King of glory came in in the form of a man, and all the dark places of Hades were lighted up.

Immediately Hades cried out: We have been conquered: woe to us! But who art thou, that hast such power and might? and what art thou, who comest here without sin who art seen to be small and yet of great power, lowly and exalted, the slave and the master, the soldier and the king, who hast power over the dead and the living? Thou wast nailed on the cross, and placed in the tomb; and now thou art free, and hast destroyed all our power. Art thou then the Jesus about whom the chief satrap Satan told us, that through cross and death thou art to inherit the whole world?

Then the King of glory seized the chief satrap Satan by the head, and delivered him to His angels, and said: With iron chains bind his hands and his feet, and his neck, and his mouth. Then He delivered him to Hades, and said: Take him, and keep him secure till my second appearing.

And Hades receiving Satan, said to him: Beelzebul, heir of fire and punishment, enemy of the saints, through what necessity didst thou bring about that the King of glory should be crucified, so that he should come here and deprive us of our power? Turn and see that not one of the dead has been left in me, but all that thou hast gained through the tree of knowledge, all hast thou lost through the tree of the cross: and all thy joy has been turned into grief; and wishing to put to death the King of glory, thou hast put thyself to death. For, since I have received thee to keep thee safe, by experience shall thou learn how many evils I shall do unto thee. O arch-devil, the beginning of death, root of sin, end of all evil, what evil didst thou find in Jesus, that thou shouldst compass his destruction? how hast thou dared to do such evil? how hast thou busied thyself to bring down such a man into this darkness, through whom thou hast been deprived of all who have died from eternity?

While Hades was thus discoursing to Satan, the King of glory stretched out His right hand, and took hold of our forefather Adam, and raised him. Then turning also to the rest, He said: Come all with me, as many as have died through the tree which he touched: for, behold, I again raise you all up through the tree of the cross. Thereupon He brought them all out, and our forefather Adam seemed to be filled with joy, and said: I thank Thy majesty, O Lord, that Thou hast brought me up out of the lowest Hades. Likewise also all the prophets and the saints said: We thank Thee, O Christ, Saviour of the world, that Thou hast brought our life up out of destruction.

And after they had thus spoken, the Saviour blessed Adam with the Sign of the Cross on his forehead, and did this also to tire patriarchs, and prophets, and martyrs, and forefathers; and He took them, and sprang up out of Hades. And while He was going, the holy fathers accompanying Him sang praises, saying: Blessed is He that cometh in the name of the Lord: Alleluia; to Him be the glory of all the saints.

And setting out to paradise, He took hold of our forefather Adam by the hand, and delivered him, and all the just, to the archangel Michael.

Step 4. Close your eyes and use rhythmic breathing to enter into meditation.

Visualize the scene you have read. Enter into it as clearly as possible, just as you entered, on Good Friday, into the scene of Our Lord's passion and death. All was lost, then: Death and Satan seemed to have triumphed.

And now we come to the turning of the tide.

See Satan, the power of evil and sin, preparing in his pride to bind the Son of God Himself. See him overthrown, and himself cast down and put into shackles by his old ally, Death. See the gates of Death torn down and broken, and all those before stepping forth into the light. And see Adam, with Eve, step out last of all, into the light of the Sun.

Michael, in esoteric tradition, is also the archangel of the Sun, and the Sun is the visible icon of Christ, the Eternal Sun. The tomb, which is the power of the material world that binds our souls, is now broken. The way forth into the Light that never fades is now open. Step with Adam, our first father, and know that he is in truth the archetype of all mankind, once fallen, now divinized.

Step 5. When you are ready, slowly release the visualization and come out of meditation as you have been instructed. Now, turn your attention to your altar. Light the candle, and unwrap the crucifix from its covering and return it to its usual place. Do this slowly and with great reverence.

Step 6. Raise your hands in the orans posture, and say:

> As in Adam, all men die, even so in Christ shall all be made alive.
>
> What God is like thee, O Lord, taking away iniquity and removing sins?
>
> Christ is our God for ever and ever, he shall be our guide, world without end.
>
> Glory be to the Father, the Son, and the Holy Spirit, as it was in the beginning, is now and forever, unto the ages of ages. Amen.

Step 7. The Collect.

> ALMIGHTY God, who through thine only-begotten Son Jesus Christ hast overcome death, and opened unto us the gate of everlasting life; We humbly beseech thee that, as by thy special grace preventing us thou dost put into our minds good desires, so by thy continual help we may bring the same to good effect; through the same Jesus Christ our Lord, who liveth and reigneth with thee and the Holy Ghost ever, one God, world without end. Amen.

CHAPTER SIX

Easter and Eastertide

Easter

Christus resurrexit. Vere, resurrexit!
Christ is risen. He is risen indeed!

Easter is the holiest day of the year, on which we celebrate the Resurrection of the Lord and the promise of eternal life.

Easter in tradition

Many of the customs that we associate with Easter are surprisingly new. The Easter Bunny, now ubiquitous in North America and elsewhere, appeared in Germany in modern times. There he was an Easter Hare, but rabbits are more common than hares in North America and hare symbolism is typically transferred to them when it crosses the Atlantic Ocean.

The Easter Bunny typically comes with colored eggs, and baskets of chocolates, candy, and presents. All of these relate, of course, to the nature of Easter as a Spring holiday and a celebration of fertility and new life. The hare or rabbit is a common symbol of Spring, and the egg is an obvious symbol of new life.

Sunrise services are very common at Easter. The symbolism of the rising Sun on the Day of the Lord's Resurrection is very powerful. If you can't attend a sunrise Mass, you can still stand in the light of the Sun, as close to sunrise as possible or immediately after awakening. Give thanks to God for the sunlight, and stand in the light for a few minutes in reverent silence.

It might be worth looking at the Easter Bunny for a moment, as he is a nice illustration of how traditions appear, how they evolve, and how often they are misunderstood.

Every year at Eastertime, certain claims start circulating on the internet about the holiday's origin. In most languages, the word for "Easter" is some variant on *Pascha*, meaning Passover. Even in English, the adjective related to Easter is "paschal," not "Easterial" or some such. Nevertheless, in English the name of the holiday was preserved from an earlier Germanic word for the same time of year. Meanwhile, there is, in one or two historical sources, a reference to a Germanic goddess named "Ostara." Very little is known about Ostara. One statue—yes, one—has been found, in Spain, bearing the name Ostara and having with it a rabbit. This statue was discovered recently after having been lost for, presumably, centuries.

Meanwhile, in a corner of Germany in the 16th or 17th century, a tradition developed in which an Easter Hare would judge the children's behavior, and reward them with colored eggs and, eventually, baskets of candy. This tradition made its way to America following the large influx of German immigrants, which began in the late 17th century.

What we think of as "paganism" in the modern world is the actual way our ancestors practiced Christianity. The ironic thing is that the notion that the traditions of the Christian world were "pagan" began with the Protestant reformers. Five centuries later, some of the descendants of these same Protestants are still insisting that Christian tradition is "really" pagan, only now they are calling themselves pagans and claiming that they are the only ones with a right to them! History is a strange thing, and the history of human ideas is the strangest thing of all.

In any case, anthropomorphic rabbits bringing children baskets filled with chocolates and hiding eggs around the house may not be ancient pagan practices, but it is a perfect example of a traditional practice, and highly encouraged.

As with Santa Claus, the gift-giver of Christmas, many people think that the day will come when they have to "Tell their children the truth" about the Easter Bunny. If you think that the day has come, be sure to tell them the real truth, which is that spirits like the Easter Bunny don't have a single physical body like we do, but instead manifest themselves everywhere people tell their stories, share their images and participate in their work.

Other Easter traditions include the lighting of bonfires—as usual.

The astrology of Easter

Easter's date is variable, but the nature of that date has an important astrological significance. The date of Easter was set as the First Sunday, after the first Full Moon, after the Spring Equinox. Each of these points has its own significance and tells us something about the nature of Easter and the Christian religion as a whole.

Sunday, as we have already discussed, is the day of the Sun. Note that the Jewish sabbath was Saturday. It is also significant that the Sun itself was darkened on Good Friday for the three hours of Our Lord's crucifixion.

The Sun, in ancient theology, is the special symbol of the celestial gods, those powers which preside over the Earth and are closer to the true Heaven than the terrestrial gods. The Sun is the ruler of the celestial gods and is especially an image of the Creator of the cosmos. Christ, the Divine Logos, is the Eternal Sun, and at this moment of His death the visible Sun is also darkened. In ancient Egypt, meanwhile, a veil was drawn across the temple at noon, because it was at this time that the Sun was at his most powerful and the gods more present.

The same solar symbolism is found in the fixing of the date *after* the Spring Equinox. In our visible world, the Equinox is the moment when the days and the nights are of equal length: after this, the days begin to increase, for the Light has triumphed over the Darkness. The moment of the Resurrection is this moment in the spiritual history of mankind.

And what of the Moon?

In the ancient understanding of the Universe, our world begins, in a certain sense, at the level of the Moon, which was the closest planet to the Earth. The visible Heavens above the Moon move in regular, ordered patterns. The Moon is changeable, her light waxing and waning, and it is below the sphere of the Moon—the ancients thought—that time and change exist. The Moon, in this sense, is also the particular ruler of Nature.

Now, the Full Moon is the moment when the Moon makes an opposition to the Sun. That is, from the perspective of the Earth, the Sun and Moon are on opposite sides, with the Earth between. From this point, the Moon begins to return to the Sun. The placement of Easter after—but not very much after—the Full Moon indicates that at this point, the natural world of which we are a part has begun the process of returning to its origin in God. Because the Full Moon is only just past, the powers of Nature, including the spirits of the natural world, are still strong, and some (though not all) of these are antagonistic toward God and man. Nevertheless, the reversal has begun, and all things are being gathered back into the Divine Mind, Christ the Word of God, from whom they sprang.

This re-gathering of all things into God is precisely the New Heaven and the New Earth of which we read in Revelation. For some, the saints, this new world is already present; for the rest of us, the journey continues.

The Esoteric meaning of Easter

Our story began on Christmas Eve with a census. "In those days, Caesar Augustus ordered a census of the entire world."

A census, let us recall, had a very specific meaning in ancient times; it was no mere bureaucratic exercise. At the census, which took place every year, or every four or seven years, every member of a given city would gather outside its walls to be counted by the censor. They would then make atonement to the God who ruled that city for the sins of its members.

At Christmas, we have a census of the entire world: Thus, we see that the story that begins is a story of atonement to a god, and that God is not the god of this or that city, or of a mountain or a sea, but the God of the entire world.

Our story continues with Jesus's baptism, which is to say, his initiation into the ancient current of power carried by John the Baptist, who tells us, "Repent, for the kingdom of Heaven is at hand." Or, to say it more correctly: Change your nous, for the kingdom of God is within you.

Jesus, revealed as the living incarnation of the Second Person of the Holy Trinity, then begins his ministry, teaching the people of Israel the Great Way of changing the nous.

On Holy Thursday, we come to the Paschal Supper. Here, several things happen. A meal is shared. The meal commemorates the Passover meal, in which the door of every Jewish household is marked by the blood of a sacrificial lamb. Thus, we know that we are about to encounter a sacrifice, and this will be the reverse of the previous Passover: Now, the Firstborn will be sacrificed, and will be the lamb, and his blood will stain the door.

"This is my flesh," he tells his disciples, "and this is my blood," distributing bread and wine among them. "It will be poured out for you and for many for the forgiveness of sins. Do this in memory of me."

In a garden, he prays. He knows what is to come. Can it be averted? If it were possible, he asks, let this cup pass from me: "But Thy will, not mine, be done."

The cup does not pass. He is arrested. Beaten, scourged, crowned with thorns. And he is sentenced to be crucified at Golgotha, the Place of the Skull.

Now, let us remember what in earlier and wiser times was known to all. The cross on which he was crucified was made from the wood of the Tree of Life itself. And the Place of the Skull is the resting place of our first parents; the skull is Adam's skull.

Now, of the three members of the soul, the nous is the highest, and its place in the subtle anatomy is in the skull. Here at the Place of the Skull, He dies upon the Tree of Life.

He descends into Hell. And there he comes in triumph; the Gate of Hell is broken, and its inmates are released.

"Take up your cross and follow me," He tells us. By sacrifice, bind yourself to the Tree of Life. Descend from the *nous* in your head to the passions burning in the hellfire of your belly, and release the energy and the will that you have bound up there in the following of earthly things. Do this, die to this world, and you will be reborn, even as He is reborn.

The Easter meditation

Preparation. Set up your altar in the usual way, with a white altar cloth. The candle you lit yesterday should be on the altar, along with vessels for incense and water for the asperges, which returns today. If you have Easter Water, you should use that. Otherwise, regular holy water will do. In a pinch, you can use water gathered from a natural source, such as rainwater, or even regular tap water blessed with the Sign of the Cross.

Step 1. Today, we will perform the complete Opening, including the asperges. Again, remember that this isn't a true opening, as the temple has remained open since Maundy Thursday.

Step 2. Standing with hands in the orans posture, say the following prayer:

> O God, who on this day through Thine only-begotten Son hast overcome Death and opened unto us the gate of everlasting Life, do thou send forth Thy Holy Spirit to guide me in my meditations and my understanding of the Resurrection of Thy Son, our Lord Jesus Christ. Amen.

Step 3. Read the following passage, the traditional Gospel reading for the day, from Mark 16:1–7:

> At that time, Mary Magdalen, and Mary, the mother of James, and Salome bought sweet spices, that coming, they might anoint Jesus. And very early in the morning, the first day of the week, they come to the sepulchre, the sun being now risen. And they said one to another: "Who shall roll us back the stone from the door of the sepulchre?" And looking, they saw the stone rolled back. For it was very great. And entering into the sepulchre, they saw a young man sitting on the right side, clothed with a white robe: and they were astonished. Who saith to them: "Be not affrighted. You seek Jesus of Nazareth, who was crucified. He is risen: he is not here. Behold the place where they laid him. But go, tell his disciples and Peter that he goeth before you into Galilee. There you shall see him, as he told you."

Step 4. Once again, take your seat and enter into meditation as you have been instructed, and visualize the scene. Imagine yourself with the women, encountering the empty tomb, and the angel, saying: "Be not afraid."

Step 5. Rise, and say the following prayer:

> This is the day the Lord hath made: Let us rejoice and be glad in it.
> Christ is risen, alleluia. Indeed, he is risen, alleluia.
> As in Adam all men died, so in Christ, all may live.

Hail thou King of Victory! Have mercy on us and save us from this world of Sin and Darkness,
Lead us to the glory of Thy Resurrection. Alleluia, Amen.

Step 6. This time, close your temple in the usual way. You may keep the candle lit if you can do so safely. Go forth in joy and gladness, and commence your Easter celebrations.

Paschaltide and the Sundays after Easter

The time after Easter is known as Paschaltide. Like Christmas, Easter is not a one-day feast, but extends over the course of the next week.

Easter is a season of rejoicing, and so it is fitting that our practice should become less structured than during Lent. If you've followed this book up to this point, you know how to meditate, to pray daily and to practice visualization where appropriate. In this section, we'll briefly go over the Sundays which follow Easter. We'll provide the Collect, which is a simple prayer that allows us to connect to the energy and intentions of the Sunday and the week that follows, and the Gospel reading. Both of these together provide an excellent source of meditation fodder for the week. (Please note that these are from the Tridentine liturgy.)

Practice during Easter time

We have already seen that the Seven Sundays of Lent and Easter reproduce the Seven Days of Creation. From Low Sunday, which is the First Sunday after Easter, to the feast of Pentecost, we have another structure of Seven Sundays. This is, then, in a sense, a Second Creation. The first set of Seven Sundays is commemorated by a fast which ends in a great feast. The second set begins in feasting and ends in something even greater: The commemoration of the descent of the Holy Spirit at Pentecost. This is, then, an image of the Second Creation of the World, which is the renewal of the world accomplished through the return of all things to their Divine Source.

Quasimodo or low Sunday

The First Sunday of Easter is called Quasimodo or Low Sunday.

Collect: O Almighty God, let our conduct and our lives always be guided by the Easter feast we have just celebrated.
Gospel: John 20:19–31

Second Sunday after Easter

Collect: You raised up our fallen world, O God, by the humiliation of Your own Son. May we, Your faithful people, be always joyful on earth, and, by being rescued from the danger of eternal death, come to everlasting happiness in heaven.
Gospel: John 10:11–16

Third Sunday after Easter

Collect: Show us the light of Your truth, O God, which guides the sinner back to the path of justice. Let we who profess to be Christians avoid whatever will endanger our faith, and follow those things which will help it.
Gospel: John 16:16–22

Fourth Sunday after Easter

Collect: O God, in whom all the faithful are united in one mind, let Your people everywhere love Your commandments and yearn for Your promises, so that, even amid the changes of this world, their hearts may always be fixed upon the true happiness of heaven.
Gospel: John 16:5–14

Fifth Sunday After Easter

Collect: O God, the source of all good, grant us Your inspiration that we may have proper thoughts, and Your guidance that we may carry them into practice.
Gospel: John 16:23–30

Note that the Fifth Sunday After Easter marks the beginning of Ascension Week. The Monday, Tuesday, and Wednesday of this week are the days of the Lesser Rogation. Turn to the chapter on the Rogation

Days in the section on the Feasts and Saints of Spring and familiarize yourself with the material there. These are days of fasting and special practice, as we prepare for the Ascension of Our Lord on Thursday.

Ascension Thursday

The Thursday of the sixth week of Easter is the Feast of the Ascension of Our Lord.

Ascension narratives

Here is how this event is described in the Gospel according to Mark, which is the traditional reading for the Feast of the Ascension:

> At that time, Jesus appeared to the eleven as they were at table: and he upbraided them with their incredulity and hardness of heart, because they did not believe them who had seen him after he was risen again. And he said to them: "Go ye into the whole world and preach the Gospel to every creature. He that believeth and is baptized shall be saved: but he that believeth not shall he condemned. And these signs shall follow them that believe: In my name they shall cast out devils. They shall speak with new tongues. They shall take up serpents: and if they shall drink any deadly thing, it shall not hurt them. They shall lay their hand upon the sick: and they shall recover."
>
> And the Lord Jesus, after he had spoken to them, was taken up into heaven and sitteth on the right hand of God. But they going forth preached everywhere: the Lord working withal, and confirming the word with signs that followed.

We see that the narrative has two parts. The first is the Great Commission to preach the Gospel to the whole world, and the second is the Ascension into Heaven. Matthew condenses the narrative, focusing only on the Great Commission:

> Now the eleven disciples went to Galilee, to the mountain to which Jesus had directed them. And when they saw him they worshiped him; but some doubted. And Jesus came and said to them, "All authority in heaven and on earth has been given to me.

> Go therefore and make disciples of all nations, baptizing them in the name of the Father and of the Son and of the Holy Spirit, teaching them to observe all that I have commanded you; and lo, I am with you always, to the close of the age."

Luke, on the other hand, gives us a summary of the Ascension in his Gospel:

> Then he led them out as far as Bethany, and lifting up his hands he blessed them. While he blessed them, he parted from them and was carried up into heaven. And they worshipped him, and returned to Jerusalem with great joy, and were continually in the temple blessing God.

In the Acts of the Apostles, however, Luke elaborates:

> So when they had come together, they asked him, "Lord, will you at this time restore the kingdom to Israel?" He said to them, "It is not for you to know times or seasons which the Father has fixed by his own authority. But you shall receive power when the Holy Spirit has come upon you; and you shall be my witnesses in Jerusalem and in all Judea and Samar'ia and to the end of the earth." And when he had said this, as they were looking on, he was lifted up, and a cloud took him out of their sight. And while they were gazing into heaven as he went, behold, two men stood by them in white robes, and said, "Men of Galilee, why do you stand looking into heaven? This Jesus, who was taken up from you into heaven, will come in the same way as you saw him go into heaven."

Notice that the Acts of the Apostles also focuses not on the Ascension alone, but on Pentecost, which is to come. This will be important soon.

Ascension in tradition

Ascension marks the completion of the cycle of the Life of Christ that began at Christmastime. The cycle begins in Advent, at the darkest time of the year, as the days grow ever shorter and we await the coming of the Winter Solstice. The date of Ascension varies year after year, but it always takes place between May 9 and June 3. This is, truly, the most joyous time of the year, when Nature is reborn but the stifling heat of summer has not yet descended, when flowers come to life and have not yet faded, when insects begin to stir but have not yet become a plague. It is always a feast, then, of Nature Reborn, the light increasing; of a new world rising out of the darkness of forgotten Winter.

The customs of Ascension tie into this seasonal symbolism in very obvious ways.

Among the most obvious is the eating of birds. The meal on Ascension Thursday should be a feast in which a bird is eaten—a chicken is the most obvious choice, though duck is tastier; North Americans might well cook a turkey out of season (and quite cheaply). The bird which flies in the air is a symbol of Heaven, and the bird eaten at the table becomes a kind of minor Communion whereby we participate in the life of Heaven.

At this time, the very first crops of the summer begin to appear. Historically, this included beans and grapes. These days, strawberries are the most obvious signs of summer, and their appearance was, indeed, taken as the sign of summer's beginning among indigenous people in the Northeastern part of what is now the United States. Most of us are not farmers, but a personal practice might involve gathering strawberries at a local farm and blessing them at dinner. Freshly picked berries are sweeter and far better than anything purchased from a store, and make a fine dessert; these may be blessed with words like the following:

> Bless + O Lord, these new fruits, gifts of the land, which Thou hast brought to maturity by the dew of heaven, by plentiful rains and by tranquil and favorable weather. Thou hast given us this fruit for our use that we may receive it with thanks in the name of our Lord, Jesus Christ. Amen.

Picnicking or hiking are very good ways to celebrate the Feast of the Ascension. At this time, the world itself is renewed, and we can celebrate the renewed world by getting out into the world of Nature. Plant life is abundant during this time, and if you know your edible plants or mushrooms well, this is a good day to go foraging. Bless the fruits of your journey with the prayer given above.

In Italy and among the Italian diaspora, it's traditional for children to catch crickets on Ascension Thursday, and this has become a custom of catching grasshoppers elsewhere. This is often quite a fun practice for children, very much worth encouraging.

The Esoteric interpretation of the Ascension

The Ascension of Jesus is the return of a single man to Heaven, and also the return of all men and all of humanity. It is accomplished once and forever in mythical time, and in historical time it is that which awaits all of us. Every person and every created thing shall ultimately be gathered back into God, the ultimate Source of all being—but how long this takes is up to us. By spiritual practice and discipline, we can hasten the end of our earthly sojourn.

Really, the only major difference between the esoteric and the mainstream perspectives on this is that the esotericist believes that the work of Return may take more than one human lifetime. Of course, within the Catholic tradition, this is also the teaching, but the Catholic Church teaches that the remaining human lifetimes will be worked out in a secondary world or condition called Purgatory, rather than reincarnation on the Earth. As always, I leave it to my readers to decide which perspective makes more sense.

Practice for Ascension

Ascension Thursday is a time to enjoy the natural world and avail ourselves of its blessings. This is a good day to go outside, take a walk or a hike, and contemplate the beauty of nature. Every visible form of beauty that we encounter in the natural world is a reflection of the Eternal Beauty which is in the Divine. Knowing this, we can turn a walk or hike into a meditation, considering how every tree or stream or sunrise is both a work of God and an image of some aspect of His nature.

In your personal practice, perform the following meditation:

Step 1. Perform the complete Opening Ritual.

Step 2. Read the texts given above, from the Gospels and the Acts of the Apostles, describing the Ascension of Our Lord.

Step 3. Visualize the scene as clearly as you can. As before, imagine yourself as both witness and participant in the Ascension of Our Lord. Know that He has gone before you, but that, in another sense, you have gone with Him. A man is ascended into Heaven and seated at the right hand of the Father, and because of this all of Humanity is, in the core of its being, in Heaven, in the presence of God.

Step 4. Slowly come out of meditation. Stand, and offer the following prayer:

Step 5. Close your meditation in the usual way.

Pentecost

We are told in Scripture that the first Pentecost took place in the Upper Room, a place which we have encountered already. In that room were the 11 remaining disciples, and also the Virgin Mary, the women of Jerusalem, and a number of other followers of Christ, totaling 120 names. We can imagine that it was quite a crowd!

The truth, as you will already have guessed, is that 120 is a symbolic number with an important significance. In ancient times, 120 was the number of Jewish colonists necessary to depart from Jerusalem and found a new city.

It is important to understand that the founding of a city was very different in ancient times. A new colony wasn't like a new suburban housing development, fabricated in a few months and with the ability to pay a mortgage the only price for admission. In the modern world, we separate the categories of "government," "residence," "family," and "religion." The ancient world understood these things differently. Governments in the ancient world, among Jews as well as pagans, were divine institutions, instituted by sacred lawgivers. The act of founding a new city was more akin to founding a church than putting up a housing subdivision, and the creation of a colony was a religious act. The creation of a new Church in the Christian tradition requires the performance of a series of rites in order to consecrate the grounds, the building, the altar, and the various other instruments involved, and the installation of relics in the altar. The founding of a new city in the ancient world was similarly involved and similarly sacred.

It was also a kind of family affair: In Greece, for example, it was expected that a new city would remain loyal to the city from which its original colonists had come, in the same way that children remain loyal to their parents even after they leave home. (This became a major issue during the Peloponnesian Wars, when the various Greek cities fought among themselves.)

Pentecost, then, represents not just a change in the ministry of the apostles or their attainment of magical abilities. It is also the founding of a new city, with all of the implications that such a thing would have had at the time.

Pentecost in tradition

In the English-speaking world, Pentecost is traditionally known as Whit Sunday. The week which followed was one of the free weeks for medieval serfs, along with the weeks after Christmas and Easter. (Note that this is more vacation time than the average American worker can expect even at a "good job" in these more enlightened times.) The day after Pentecost is Whit Monday, which remained a public holiday in the United Kingdom until very recently. Whit Monday was a time for public parades and religious processions, and also a day when children were given a new set of clothes.

America is notoriously bad at holidays, and the UK abandoned Whit Monday in the 1970s, but we can still incorporate elements of the old feast into our homes and our lives. Pentecost always comes at or near the end of the school year, and so this could be a fine time to present children with gifts of clothing suitable for the summer. On Pentecost or Whitsunday itself, of course, you should either attend appropriate church services or perform a ritual of your own, at home. This should include reading the second chapter of the Acts of the Apostles, in which the first Pentecost is recounted.

If you are working with the initiatory aspect of this book, you can now proceed to the Initiation of Pentecost, which concludes this work.

The initiation of Pentecost

Step 1. Open a magical temple in the usual way. You should have a white cloth on the altar.

Step 2. With hands in the orans posture, say the words:

> Our help is in the Name of the Lord,
> Who hath made the Heavens and the Earth.
> May the Lord be with me this day and guide the work of my hands, the speech of my tongue, and the thoughts of my heart as I enter into this work of initiation.

Step 3. From your preferred Bible translation, read the Acts of the Apostles, Chapter 2. This is the account of the first Pentecost.

Step 4. Close your eyes and use rhythmic breathing to enter into meditation. When you are ready, visualize the scene you have just read. Bear in mind the details given earlier in this chapter. The 11 apostles are joined by the Blessed Virgin Mary and the women of Jerusalem, as well as a great crowd of believers. Imagine that you yourself are among the 120, one of those who will now go forth to found the City of God throughout the world. See the Holy Spirit descending like tongues of fire upon all those in the room, feel yourself transformed, and, with the others, go forth into the streets to preach to all those you encounter.

Step 5. When you are ready, come out of meditation. Stand with your hands in the orans posture, and say the following words:

> On this day of Pentecost, I pray:
> Come, Holy Spirit, fill the hearts of thy faithful, and enkindle in them the fire of thy love.

Imagine the light pouring down from Heaven. It arrives at the crown of your head, where it forms a golden sphere of light. From this sphere it continues, filling the central column of your body, expanding and filling your physical body, your energetic body, and your astral body with holy light.

Say:

> Thou shalt send forth thy spirit and they shall be created, and thou shalt renew the face of the Earth.

Now, imagine the light continues, extending down through the soles of your feet, all the way down into the heart of the Earth. At the same time, it expands, so that a circle of light extends outward in every direction. Imagine this as a holy, healing light, bringing order, beauty and harmony to the people, abundance and fertility to the land, and blessings to all who are able to receive them.

Say:

> Oh God who didst instruct the apostles in the Holy Spirit, grant in that same Spirit that we may be truly wise, and rejoice in His consolations always.

Bring your hands together in the "prayer position" at your heart. As you do so, return your attention to the sphere of light at the crown of your head and feel it descend into your body, into your heart. Slowly chant the word:

> *AMEN.*

> Feel and know that the light of the Holy Spirit is there at your heart, illuminating your being, able to be called upon whenever you need guidance, healing, or consolation.

Step 6. Close your temple in the usual way.

AFTERWORD

The Initiation of Pentecost is the conclusion of our journey in this book, but, like all initiations, it is only the beginning of the work. Remember that the very word *initiatio* means "a beginning." A martial arts instructor I once knew used to say that "The day you receive your black belt is the day you become able to start learning." Every initiation follows this same pattern. Now that you have received your initiation, you have truly begun the journey.

You may wish to look back over the material in this book, and especially to review the notes that you have made in your meditation journal. Consider them again from your current point of view, and see if anything new jumps out at you.

If this is the first book of Sacramental Magic you have read, you may wish to explore the previous books in this series, especially *The Book of Sacramental Magic* itself. God willing, further books will explore the remaining traditions of Springtime, including the many saints and feast days which we have had to leave aside for now, and continue through the seasons of summer, the Feast of Saint Michael, and the Dark Triduum of Halloween, All Saints Day, and All Souls Day. May God bless you and keep you until then.

APPENDIXES

Appendix 1: Sources and further reading

The following volumes are mostly concerned with Christian tradition, both exoteric and esoteric, and all have informed the writing of this book.

Exoteric Christianity

The Liturgical Year by Dom Prosper Gueranger

Gueranger was a 19th-century French priest and Dominican monk. His great work, *The Liturgical Year*, spans 15 volumes and covers the year of the Church in minute detail, from Advent onward. The complete set can be very expensive, but most of it is available online.

The Saint Andrew Daily Missal, with Vespers for Sundays and Feasts by Dom Gaspar Lefebvre

This is a 1925 English missal, including the propers of the Mass for every Sunday of the year in both English and Latin. If you are working within a Roman Catholic tradition, this will provide you with the propers for the home Mass throughout the year. This is a big book, a century old now, and physical copies can be expensive. Fortunately, as it is 100 years old, electronic copies can easily (and legally) be found online.

The Rituale Romanum

The Rituale is the Catholic Church's official book of rites for both the Sacraments and sacramentals. If you can read Latin, you can find very old editions on websites like archive.org. St Cyprian's Press has also released a complete translation in formal, Elizabethan English, rather than the pedestrian English of modern translations. It is available online at https://www.lulu.com/shop/editors-of-saint-cyprian-press/the-roman-ritual-the-blessings-processions-litanies/paperback/product-149r9qgz.html.

The Easter Book by Francis X. Weiser

The follow-up to Weiser's earlier volume, *The Christmas Book*, this is a very useful compilation of Lent and Easter traditions from around the world.

Catholic Customs and Traditions: A Popular Guide by Greg Dues

Published in 1983, this is a detailed look at Catholic traditions throughout the year, a useful companion to the works of Francis Weiser.

Esoteric Christianity

Three Books of Occult Philosophy by Cornelius Agrippa

These books were originally written in 1531. Agrippa's goal was to synthesize the entire esoteric (or "occult") philosophical tradition, from ancient times to what was to him the present day. The 1651 English translation is available for free online, but Eric Purdue's 2021 translation is worth every penny you will spend on it.

Rosicrucian Cosmo-Conception by Max Heindel

Written in 1925, this is a very different sort of book, at once deeply devout and totally radical. The Rosicrucian tradition approaches Christianity through the lens of the esoteric tradition, especially as formulated in the 19th and early 20th centuries.

The Experience of the Inner Worlds by Gareth Knight

Knight was at once a devout Anglican and an esotericist in the tradition of Dion Fortune, and this book provides a gentle and effective introduction to the traditions of Christian magic.

The Magic of Catholicism by Brother A.D.A.

It can be said that the system of Sacramental Magic, which I have presented in this and other books, begins with occult philosophy and works outward toward Catholic practice. This book, and its author, takes the opposite approach: beginning with Catholic doctrine and working outward toward magical practice. Somehow, the place we arrive looks very similar, and this book and its companions (available on the author's website at www.thauvmapub.org) are highly recommended.

The Kybalion by "The Three Initiates"

The Kybalion is one of those odd texts which is not at all what it claims to be, but which is immensely useful nonetheless. It claims to be a treatise on the Hermetic philosophy of ancient (or late Classical) Egypt; in fact, it's a synthesis of 19th-century occult philosophy and New Thought. "The Three Initiates," who are supposed to have written it, are actually the American New Thought guru William Walker Atkinson.

Mystical Meditations on the Christian collects by Dion Fortune

The last century produced a number of great esoteric thinkers, magicians and occultists, but Dion Fortune was probably the greatest. She wrote a large number of works on magic, Cabala, and occult philosophy, all of which are worth careful study. I've chosen to include the *Mystical Meditations on the Collects* in particular as another example of the application of occult philosophy to the Sacramental Christian tradition.

Appendix 2: A selection of common prayers

Here is a set of common prayers which you may wish to use as part of your practice. All of these can be said any time, or they can be prayed as part of your daily practice. Many are suitable as "closing prayers" for the rituals given. Many people like to pray in Latin, and I've included Latin versions of many of the prayers, as well as Latin versions of prayers you most likely know already.

The Lord's prayer

Latin:

> PATER NOSTER, qui es in caelis, sanctificetur nomen tuum. Adveniat regnum tuum. Fiat voluntas tua, sicut in caelo et in terra. Panem nostrum quotidianum da nobis hodie, et dimitte nobis debita nostra sicut et nos dimittimus debitoribus nostris. Et ne nos inducas in tentationem, sed libera nos a malo. Amen.

English:

> OUR FATHER, who art in heaven, hallowed be thy name. Thy kingdom come, thy will be done, on earth as it is in heaven. Give us this day our daily bread, and forgive us our trespasses, as we forgive those who trespass against us. And lead us not into temptation, but deliver us from evil, [for thine is the kingdom, the power and the glory, for ever and ever.] Amen.

Hail Mary

Latin:

> AVE MARIA, gratia plena, Dominus tecum. Benedicta tu in mulieribus, et benedictus fructus ventris tui, Iesus. Sancta Maria, Mater Dei, ora pro nobis peccatoribus, nunc, et in hora mortis nostrae. Amen.

English:

> HAIL MARY, full of grace, the Lord is with thee. Blessed art thou among women, and blessed is the fruit of thy womb, Jesus.

Holy Mary, Mother of God, pray for us sinners, now, and at the hour of our death. Amen.

Glory Be

Latin:

GLORIA PATRI, et Filio, et Spiritui Sancto. Sicut erat in principio, et nunc, et semper, et in saecula saeculorum. Amen.

English:

GLORY BE to the Father, and to the Son, and to the Holy Spirit. As it was in the beginning, is now and forever, unto the ages of ages. Amen.

The Holy Spirit prayer

Latin:

VENI, Sáncte Spíritus, reple tuorum corda fidelium, et tui amóris in eis ignem accende. V. Emitte Spíritum tuum et creabuntur; R. Et renovabis faciem terrae.

Oremus: DEUS, qui corda fidelium Sancti Spíritus illustratione docuisti. Da nobis in eodem Spiritu recta sapere, et de eius semper consolatione gaudere. Per Christum Dominum nostrum. Amen.

English:

Come, Holy Spirit, fill the hearts of Thy faithful and enkindle in them the fire of Thy love. Send forth Thy Spirit and they shall be created, and Thou shalt renew the face of the earth.

Let us pray.

O God, Who didst instruct the hearts of the faithful by the light of the Holy Spirit, grant us in the same Spirit to be truly wise, and ever to rejoice in His consolation, through Christ, our Lord. Amen.

Magnificat

Latin:

Magnificat anima mea Dominum;
et exultavit spíritus meus in Deo salutari meo,
quia respexit humilitatem ancillae suæ;
Ecce enim ex hoc beatam me dicent omnes generationes.
quia fecit mihi magna, qui potens est, et sanctum nomen eius,
Et misericordia eius a progenie in progenies timentibus eum.
Fecit potentiam in brachio suo;
dispersit superbos mente cordis sui;
deposuit potentes de sede, et exaltavit humiles;
esurientes implevit bonis
et divites dimisit inanes.
Suscepit Israel puerum suum, recordatus misericordiae suæ,
sicut locutus est ad patres nostros,
Abraham et semini eius in saecula.

English:

My soul doth magnify the Lord.
And my spirit hath rejoiced in God my Savior.
For he hath regarded: the lowliness of his handmaiden: For behold, from henceforth: all generations shall call me blessed.
For he that is mighty hath magnified me: and holy is his Name.
And his mercy is on them that fear him: throughout all generations.
He hath shewed strength with his arm: he hath scattered the proud in the imagination of their hearts.
He hath put down the mighty from their seat: and hath exalted the humble and meek.
He hath filled the hungry with good things: and the rich he hath sent empty away.
He remembering his mercy hath holpen his servant Israel:
As he promised to our forefathers, Abraham and his seed for ever.

Hail, Holy Queen

Hail, Holy Queen, Mother of Mercy,
our life, our sweetness and our hope.

To thee do we cry,
poor banished children of Eve.
To thee do we send up our sighs,
mourning and weeping in this valley of tears.
Turn then, most gracious advocate,
thine eyes of mercy toward us,
and after this our exile
show unto us the blessed fruit of thy womb, Jesus.
O clement, O loving,
O sweet Virgin Mary.

Saint Michael prayer

Latin:

Sáncte Míchael Archángele, defénde nos in proélio, cóntra nequítiam et insídias diáboli ésto præsídium. Ímperet ílli Déus, súpplices deprecámur: tuque, prínceps milítiæ cæléstis, Sátanam aliósque spíritus malígnos, qui ad perditiónem animárum pervagántur in múndo, divína virtúte, in inférnum detrúde. Ámen.

English:

Saint Michael the Archangel, defend us in battle. Be our protection against the malice and snares of the devil. May God rebuke him we humbly pray; and do thou, O Prince of the Heavenly host, by the power of God, thrust into Hell Satan and all evil spirits who wander through the world for the ruin of souls. Amen.

Guardian angel prayer

Angel of God, my guardian dear,
To whom God's love commits me here,
Ever this day (night) be at my side,
To light and guard, to rule and guide. Amen.

Fatima prayer

O My Jesus, forgive us our sins, save us from the fires of Hell, lead all souls to Heaven, especially those in most need of Thy mercy.

Prayer of Saint Francis

> Lord, make me a channel of thy peace!
> That where there is hatred,
> I may bring love.
> That where there is wrong,
> I may bring the spirit of forgiveness.
> That where there is discord,
> I may bring harmony.
> That where there is error,
> I may bring truth.
> That where there is doubt,
> I may bring faith.
> That where there is despair,
> I may bring hope.
> That where there are shadows,
> I may bring light.
> That where there is sadness,
> I may bring joy.
> Lord, grant that I may seek rather to comfort,
> than to be comforted.
> To understand,
> than to be understood.
> To love,
> than to be loved.
> For it is by self-forgetting that one finds.
> It is by forgiving that one is forgiven.
> It is by dying that one awakens to eternal life.

Three Lenten hymns in Latin and English

The following hymns are sung during Passiontide and Holy Week. In your personal practice, they may be sung or chanted, in English or in Latin, as a form of meditation.

Pange Lingua Gloriosi

This is a Lenten hymn traditionally sung on Maundy Thursday. The English translation is by Edward Caswell.

Latin:

> *Pange, lingua, gloriósi Córporis mystérium,*
> *Sanguinísque pretiósi, Quem in mundi prétium*
> *Fructus ventris generósi Rex effúdit géntium.*
>
> *Nobis datus, nobis natus Ex intácta Vírgine,*
> *Et in mundo conversátus, Sparso verbi sémine,*
> *Sui moras incolátus Miro clausit órdine.*
>
> *In suprémæ nocte coenæ Recúmbens cum frátribus*
> *Observáta lege plene Cibis in legálibus,*
> *Cibum turbæ duodénæ Se dat suis mánibus.*
>
> *Verbum caro, panem verum Verbo carnem éfficit:*
> *Fitque sanguis Christi merum, Et si sensus déficit,*
> *Ad firmándum cor sincérum Sola fides súfficit.*
>
> *Tantum ergo sacraméntum Venerémur cérnui:*
> *Et antíquum documéntum Novo cedat rítui:*
> *Præstet fides suppleméntum Sénsuum deféctui.*
>
> *Genitóri, Genitóque Laus et jubilátio,*
> *Salus, honor, virtus quoque Sit et benedíctio:*
> *Procedénti ab utróque Compar sit laudátio.*
> *Amen.*

English:

Sing, my tongue, the Saviour's glory, Of His Flesh, the Mystery sing;
Of the Blood, all price exceeding, Shed by our Immortal King,
Destined, for the world's Redemption, From a noble Womb to spring.

Of a pure and spotless Virgin Born for us on earth below,
He, as Man, with man conversing, Stayed, the seeds of truth to sow;
Then He closed in solemn order Wondrously His Life of woe.

On the night of that Last Supper, Seated with His chosen band,
He, the Paschal Victim eating, First fulfils the Law's command;
Then as Food to all his brethren Gives Himself with His own Hand.

Word-made-Flesh, the bread of nature By His Word to Flesh He turns;
Wine into His Blood He changes: What though sense no change discerns.
Only be the heart in earnest, Faith her lesson quickly learns.

Down in adoration falling, Lo, the sacred Host we hail,
Lo, o'er ancient forms departing Newer rites of grace prevail:
Faith for all defects supplying, When the feeble senses fail.

To the Everlasting Father And the Son who comes on high
With the Holy Ghost proceeding Forth from each eternally,
Be salvation, honor, blessing, Might and endless majesty.
Amen.

Stabat Mater

A hymn of the Virgin Mary, this was traditionally sung on the Friday of Sorrows, and now often accompanies the Stations of the Cross.

Latin:

Stabat mater dolorósa, juxta Crucem lacrimósa, dum pendébat Fílius.

Cuius ánimam geméntem, contristántem et doléntem pertransívit gládius.
O quam tristis et afflícta fuit illa benedícta, mater Unigéniti!

Quae mœrébat et dolébat, pia Mater, dum vidébat nati pœnas ínclyti.

Quis est homo qui non fleret, matrem Christi si vidéret in tanto supplício?

Quis non posset contristári Christi Matrem contemplári doléntem cum Fílio?

Pro peccátis suæ gentis vidit Jésum in torméntis, et flagéllis súbditum.

Vidit suum dulcem Natum moriéndo desolátum, dum emísit spíritum.
Eja, Mater, fons amóris me sentíre vim dolóris fac, ut tecum lúgeam.

Fac, ut árdeat cor meum in amándo Christum Deum ut sibi compláceam.

Sancta Mater, istud agas, crucifíxi fige plagas cordi meo válide.

Tui Nati vulneráti, tam dignáti pro me pati, pœnas mecum dívide.

Fac me tecum pie flere, crucifíxo condolére, donec ego víxero.

Juxta Crucem tecum stare, et me tibi sociáre in planctu desídero.

Virgo vírginum præclára, mihi iam non sis amára, fac me tecum plángere.

Fac ut portem Christi mortem, passiónis fac consórtem, et plagas recólere.

Fac me plagis vulnerári, fac me Cruce inebriári, et cruóre Fílii.

Flammis ne urar succénsus, per te, Virgo, sim defénsus in die iudícii.

Christe, cum sit hinc exire, da per Matrem me veníre ad palmam victóriæ.

Quando corpus moriétur, fac, ut ánimæ donétur paradísi glória.

Amen.

English:

At the Cross her station keeping,
Stood the mournful Mother weeping,
Close to Jesus to the last:

Through her heart, his sorrow sharing,
All his bitter anguish bearing,
now at length the sword has pass'd.

Oh, how sad and sore distress'd
Was that Mother highly blest
Of the sole-begotten One!

Christ above in torment hangs;
She beneath beholds the pangs
Of her dying glorious Son.

Is there one who would not weep,
Whelm'd in miseries so deep,
Christ's dear Mother to behold?

Can the human heart refrain
From partaking in her pain,
In that Mother's pain untold?

Bruis'd, derided, curs'd, defil'd,
She beheld her tender Child
All with bloody scourges rent;

For the sins of his own nation,
Saw Him hang in desolation,
Till His Spirit forth He sent.

O thou Mother! fount of love!
Touch my spirit from above,
Make my heart with thine accord:

Make me feel as thou hast felt;
Make my soul to glow and melt
With the love of Christ my Lord.

Holy Mother! pierce me through;
In my heart each wound renew
Of my Saviour crucified:

Let me share with thee His pain,
Who for all my sins was slain,
Who for me in torments died.

Let me mingle tears with thee,
Mourning Him who mourn'd for me,
All the days that I may live:

By the Cross with thee to stay;
There with thee to weep and pray;
Is all I ask of thee to give.

Virgin of all virgins blest!,
Listen to my fond request:
Let me share thy grief divine;

Let me, to my latest breath,
In my body bear the death
Of that dying Son of thine.

Wounded with his every wound,
Steep my soul till it hath swoon'd,
In His very blood away;

Be to me, O Virgin, nigh,
Lest in flames I burn and die,
In his awful Judgment day.

Christ, when Thou shalt call me hence,
Be Thy Mother my defence,
Be Thy Cross my victory;

While my body here decays,
May my soul thy goodness praise,
Safe in Paradise with Thee.

Misererei Mei

This is the 51st Psalm, which is sung during Tenebrae services on Spy Wednesday or Maundy Thursday. The best-known setting was composed by Gregorio Allegri in the 17th century. Find a copy online and listen to it; you will thank me. The English translation is the Douay-Rheims version of this psalm.

> *Miserere mei, Deus, secundum magnam misericordiam tuam;*
> *et secundum multitudinem miserationum tuarum, dele iniquitatem meam.*
>
> *Amplius lava me ab iniquitate mea,*
> *et a peccato meo munda me.*
>
> *Quoniam iniquitatem meam ego cognosco,*
> *et peccatum meum cóntra me est semper.*
>
> *Tibi soli peccavi, et malum coram te feci;*
> *ut justificeris in sermonibus tuis,*
> *et vincas cum judicaris.*
>
> *Ecce enim in iniquitatibus conceptus sum,*
> *et in peccátis concepit me mater mea.*
>
> *Ecce enim veritatem dilexisti;*
> *incerta et occulta sapientiæ tuæ manifestasti mihi.*

APPENDIXES

Asperges me hyssopo, et mundabor;
lavabis me, et super nivem dealbabor.

Auditui meo dabis gaudium et lætitiam,
et exsultabunt ossa humiliata.

Averte faciem tuam a peccátis meis,
et omnes iniquitates meas dele.

Cor mundum crea in me, Deus,
et spíritum rectum innova in visceribus meis.

Ne projicias me a facie tua,
et spíritum sanctum tuum ne auferas a me.

Redde mihi lætitiam salutaris tui,
et spiritu principali confirma me.

Docebo iniquos vias tuas,
et impii ad te convertentur.

Libera me de sanguinibus, Deus, Deus salutis meæ,
et exsultabit lingua mea justitiam tuam.

Domine, labia mea aperies,
et os meum annuntiabit laudem tuam.

Quoniam si voluisses sacrificium, dedissem utique;
holocaustis non delectaberis.

Sacrificium Deo spíritus contribulatus;
cor contritum et humiliatum, Deus, non despicies.

Benigne fac, Domine, in bona voluntate tua Sion,
ut ædificentur muri Jerusalem.

Tunc acceptabis sacrificium justitiæ, oblationes et holocausta;
tunc imponent super altare tuum vitulos.

English:

Have mercy on me, O God, according to thy great mercy.
And according to the multitude of thy tender mercies blot out my iniquity.

Wash me yet more from my iniquity, and cleanse me from my sin.
For I know my iniquity, and my sin is always before me.

To thee only have I sinned, and have done evil before thee: that thou mayst be justified in thy words and mayst overcome when thou art judged.
For behold I was conceived in iniquities; and in sins did my mother conceive me.
For behold thou hast loved truth: the uncertain and hidden things of thy wisdom thou hast made manifest to me.
Thou shalt sprinkle me with hyssop, and I shall be cleansed: thou shalt wash me, and I shall be made whiter than snow.
To my hearing thou shalt give joy and gladness: and the bones that have been humbled shall rejoice.

Turn away thy face from my sins, and blot out all my iniquities.
Create a clean heart in me, O God: and renew a right spirit within my bowels.
Cast me not away from thy face; and take not thy holy spirit from me.
Restore unto me the joy of thy salvation, and strengthen me with a perfect spirit.
I will teach the unjust thy ways: and the wicked shall be converted to thee.

Deliver me from blood, O God, thou God of my salvation: and my tongue shall extol thy justice.
O Lord, thou wilt open my lips: and my mouth shall declare thy praise.
For if thou hadst desired sacrifice, I would indeed have given it: with burnt offerings thou wilt not be delighted.
A sacrifice to God is an afflicted spirit: a contrite and humbled heart, O God, thou wilt not despise.
Deal favourably, O Lord, in thy good will with Sion; that the walls of Jerusalem may be built up.

Then shalt thou accept the sacrifice of justice, oblations and whole burnt offerings: then shall they lay calves upon thy altar.

Appendix 3: An Easter Calendar

2026

Septuagesima: February 1; Ash Wednesday: February 18; Easter: April 5; Ascension: May 14; Pentecost: May 24

2027

Septuagesima: January 24; Ash Wednesday: February 10; Easter: March 28; Ascension: May 6; Pentecost: May 16

2028

Septuagesima: February 13; Ash Wednesday: March 1; Easter: April 16; Ascension: May 25; Pentecost: June 4

2029

Septuagesima: January 28; Ash Wednesday: February 14; Easter: April 1; Ascension: May 10; Pentecost: May 20

2030

Septuagesima: February 17; Ash Wednesday: March 6; Easter: April 21; Ascension: May 30; Pentecost: June 9

2031

Septuagesima: February 9; Ash Wednesday: February 26; Easter: April 13; Ascension: May 22; Pentecost: June 1

2032

Septuagesima: January 25; Ash Wednesday: February; 11 Easter: March; 28 Ascension: May 6; Pentecost: May 16

2033

Septuagesima: February 13; Ash Wednesday: March 2; Easter: April 17; Ascension: May 26; Pentecost: June 5

2034

Septuagesima: February 5; Ash Wednesday: February 22; Easter: April 9; Ascension: May 21; Pentecost: May 28

2035

Septuagesima: January 21; Ash Wednesday: February 7; Easter: March 25; Ascension: May 3; Pentecost: May 13

2036

Septuagesima: February 10; Ash Wednesday: February 27; Easter: April 13; Ascension: May 22; Pentecost: June 1

2037

Septuagesima: February 1; Ash Wednesday: February 18; Easter: April 5; Ascension: May 14; Pentecost: May 24

2038

Septuagesima: February 21; Ash Wednesday: March 10; Easter: April 25; Ascension: June 3; Pentecost: June 13

2039

Septuagesima: February 6; Ash Wednesday: February 23; Easter: April 10; Ascension: May 19; Pentecost: May 29

2040

Septuagesima: January 29; Ash Wednesday: February 15; Easter: April 1; Ascension: May 10; Pentecost: May 20

BIBLIOGRAPHY

Page 42 – Gueranger, Dom Prosper. *The Liturgical Year, Volume 5: Lent.* Accessed online at http://www.liturgialatina.org/

Page 43 – The selection from *The Kybalion* is from Atkinson, William Walker, writing as The Three Initiates, *The Kybalion*. Chicago, The Yogi Publication Society, 1912.

Page 87 – Plato, *Timaeus*.

Page 112 – The selection from *The Gospel of Nicodemus* comes from *The Lost Books of the Bible*, edited by Rutherford H. Platt, Jr., 1926

Dues, Greg. *Catholic Customs and Traditions*, 1983.

Weiser, Francis X. *The Easter Book*, 1982.

INDEX

abstinence, 50
    from alcohol, 51
    from meat, 50–51, 53
active force, 98–99
active imagination. *See* visualization
Adam, 63, 124, 125
Advent, 32, 46
Agrippa, C., 146
Air element, 71–72, 73
Air-oriented charity, 73
Alighieri, D. *See* Dante Alighieri
almsgiving, 56–57
altar, 13, 24
    cloths, 14–15, 24
angels, 6, 72
Angelus, 18
Annunciation, 3
archangels, 72, 79
Aristotle, 78, 81
Ascension, 31. *See also* Paschaltide
    esoteric interpretation, 138
    feast, 135–136
    and Pentecost, 1–2

    practice for, 138–139
    Thursday, 135
    in tradition, 136–138
    Week, 134
Ash Wednesday, 30, 62
    atonement, 62–63
    becoming Christ, 63
    blessing of Ashes, 65–66
    calcining, 64
    consecrated ash on forehead, 62, 63
    Divine, 63
    dust, 63
    in esoteric Christianity, 63–64
    Gospel reading, 66
    ritual, 64–65, 66–67
    sackcloth, 62
    third eye, 62
Astral Plane. *See* soul—plane of
astrologers, 90
Atkinson, W. W., 147
atonement, 62–63
Saint Augustine, 72
axis mundi, 77

Bacchus, 9
banishing rituals, 19
Banishing Sign of the Cross, 19
beers in Western world, 51
Bible, 15
    canonical Gospels, 11
    concept of "day", 31–32
    gods, 90
    King James Bible, 5
    translations, 12–13
    21st Psalm, 111
Binah, 98
bodies, 119
The Book of Sacramental Magic (Thomas), 17
Brand Sunday, 67, 69
"the bread of Life", 94
Brother, A.D.A., 147
Burial of Winter, 87–88

Caiaphas, 98
calcining, 64
Candles, 14
canonical Gospels, 11
Carnival, 40–41
Caswell, E., 152
Catholic Customs and Traditions (Dues), 146
Chaos, 12. *See also* planes
Cheesefare, 38. *See also* Quinquegesima
Chokhma, 98
Christ (Jesus), 87, 125. *See also* God
    Ascension, 136
    baptism, 130
    becoming Christ, 63
    courage of, 23
    dating Christ's nativity, 119
    Divine Mind, 100
    exorcism, 85
    fasting to imitate, 52–53
    feet washing, 110
    healing mercy, 44
    icon/symbol of, 34, 125, 129
    manger as cave, 76
    as New Adam, 64, 106
    as new human, 63
    only-begotten Son, 125
    palm ash, 63
    passion, 98, 99, 101
    passive, 98
    and plane of Ideas, 11
    providence of, 100
    purification and incarnation, 63, 130
    and red colour, 15
    resurrection of, 1, 3, 9, 79
    revealing His Glory, 79
    Second Person of the Holy Trinity, 130
    temptation of, 68
    transfiguration of, 77, 78, 102
    True Adam, 81
    true sacrifice revealed in, 94
    Word of God, 130
Christianity
    banishing ritual, 19
    central moment in, 1
    Eastern Orthodox Christian, 8
    esoteric, 3, 10
    European Christendom, 10–11
    magic and Mysteries, 3
    mainstream churches, 10
    as Mystery religion, 9
    and pagan world, 2
    Sacramental churches, 10
    true initiation, 32
Christian magic foundation, 4, 17, 18, 19, 20–22. *See also* Banishing Sign of the Cross
    banishing rituals, 19
    closing ritual, 26–27
    daily prayer, 18, 35
    lectio divina, 22, 23
    magical temple, 24
    meditation, 22
    opening ritual, 25–26
    required pieces of equipment, 24–25
    sacred language, 20
    Sphere of Protection, 21
    vibration, 20
    visualization, 19–20

Christmas
    abstinence, 50
    Adam–Eve, 63
    almsgiving, 56–57
    cave, 76
    Confiteor Ritual, 59
    Via Dolorosa, 59–60
    effects of confession, 59
    feasts following, 46
    imitation of Christ, 63
    Winter Solstice, 46
Church, 6
    mainstream churches, 10
    The Mass, 7
collective energies, 5
Communion with Divine, 10
confession, 10
    Anglican General, 43–44
    effects of, 59
confirmation, 8
Confiteor
    Liberal Catholic, 44
    Ritual, 59
    Roman Catholic, 43
consciousness, changes in, 6–7
Cóntra Celsum (Origen), 62
creation, 32
    first, 32
    Fourth Day of Creation, 89–92
    -Lent meditation tools, 13–15
    Second Creation, 133
    six Sundays of, 45
    of Sun and Stars, 91
    Sunday as Seventh Day of, 81
Cross, stations of the, 60
crucifix, 13
cult, 9
Cybele, 9

Dante Alighieri, 11, 22
"day", concept of, 31–32
Dead Sunday, 86
desolation, 69
devil, 11
Dion Fortune, 147
St. Dionysius the Areopagite, 11

disenchantment of world, 2
Divine Comedy (Dante Alighieri), 22
Divine Mind. *See* mind, plane of
Divine Names (St. Dionysius the Areopagite), 11
Divine Plane. *See* unity, plane of
divine reading. *See lectio divina*
divine simplicity, 49
doppelbock, 30–31
Douay-Rheims, 5, 12, 15, 157
dryness, 69
Dues, G., 146

Easter, 29, 31, 33, 46, 48, 127, 133.
        See also Paschaltide;
        Pentecost
    astrology, 129–130
    bunny, 129
    calendar, 160–163
    cycle builds on Christmas cycle, 3
    esoteric meaning, 130–131
    fate, 1
    feast, 31
    hare, 128
    Lenten practices, 49
    meditation, 131–133
    Monday, 1
    repentance, 58–59
    Sacramental Confession, 59
    stations of the Cross, 60
    structure of, 31–32
    Sunday as Seventh Day
        of creation, 81
    traditions, 3, 127–129
    Triduum, 48, 109–110, 111–112
    Water, 118
    The way of the Cross meditation,
        60–61
The Easter Book (Weiser), 146
egregore, 11, 39. *See also* collective
        energies
Elijah, 79
Energetic Plane. *See* energy, plane of
energy, plane of, 11–12
epithymia, 52
Equinox, 129

Etheric Plane. *See* energy, plane of
    magic, 7, 11
    spirits, 84
exorcism, 83–85
"exoteric", 10
The Experience of the Inner Worlds (Knight), 147
"eye of the soul", 62

fasting, 52–55. *See also* Lenten Fast
Fatima Prayer, 23, 27, 151
firmament, 74, 75, 76
Fontana, 86
forces in Universe, 98–99
Forgiveness Sunday, 38–39. *See also* Quinquegesima
fourfold breath, 23
40-day fast, 29
Franciscan theory of the Atonement, 3
Francis, Prayer of Saint, 23, 27, 40, 152
Freya, 21
Friday of Sorrows, 103

Genesis, 74
German Beer Laws, 51
Gesimatide (pre-Lent), 3, 14, 17, 30, 42, 49, 68, 97. *See also* Quinquegesima; Septuagesima; Sexagesima; Shrove Tuesday
    and carnival, 40–41
    purposes, 33
    spiritual alchemy, 33
Gibson, M., 97
Glory Be, 18, 27, 125, 149
God(s), 70, 90, 93. *See also* Christ (Jesus)
    as all-good Creator, 78
    ALMIGHTY God, 125
    in ancient paganism, 78
    of ancient world, 9, 78
    becoming like, 70
    God Most High, 90
    God's will, 49
    I AM, 102, 103
    Lent as God's creation, 45
    over material universe, 93–94
    evil, 78–79
    message from, 72
    messengers, 94
    philosophers on, 78
    reliance on, 70
    sacrifice and, 78, 94
    uncreated, 93
Goddess, 9
    Ostara, 128
    Persephone, 9
Golden Dawn's pentagram, 21
Golgotha, journey to, 60
Good Friday, 115. *See also* Holy Week
    meditation, 117–118
    Seven Last Words, 116–117
    Three Holy Hours, 116
The Gospel of Nicodemus (Platt, Jr.), 11, 13, 121
Guardian angel prayer, 151
Gueranger, D. P., 46, 145

Hades, 9, 118, 119, 120
    and Satan, 121–124
Hail, Holy Queen, 150–151
Hail Mary, 18, 148–149
Harrowing of Hell, 11, 118–120
"Heavens", 90–91
Heindel, M., 146
Henadic plane. *See* unity, plane of
Hera, 21
Herod, 90
High Magic, 7
Holy Saturday, 118. *See also* Holy Week
    Easter Water, 118
    Harrowing of Hell, 118–120
    meditation, 120–125
Holy Spirit, 6, 11
    Pentecost and, 31, 32
    prayer, 23, 50, 73, 149
Holy Trinity, 12, 21
holy water container, 13
Holy Week, 105. *See also* Good Friday; Holy Saturday; Maundy Thursday
    meditations, 109
    Spy Wednesday, 110
Homer, 22, 78
homo, 63

INDEX 169

I AM, 102, 103
Ideas, plane of, 11
incarnation
    Christ, 63, 130
    escape from, 120
incense container, 14
Inferno (Dante Alighieri), 11
initiates
    to energies of Easter season, 4
    of Mystery, 9
    purification of, 53
initiation, 8–9
    rituals of, 10
    wandering in desert, 69
Intellectual Plane. *See* mind, plane of
Invocabit Sunday, 67

John the Baptist, 58, 83, 130
journal and pen, 15
Jupiter, 119

Kingdom of Heaven, 35
King James Bible, 5
Knight, G., 147
The Kybalion (Atkinson), 47, 48, 147

Laetare Sunday, 86, 88, 95
Last Supper, 110
law of rhythm, 47–48
lectio divina, 22, 38
Lefebvre, D. G., 145
Lent, 30, 31, 33, 45. *See also* Ash
    Wednesday; Easter; Passion
    Sunday; Pentecost; temptation
    becoming like God, 70
    divine simplicity, 49
    Easter Sunday, 81
    ember fast, 72–73
    firmament, 74, 75, 76
    foods, 30–31
    Fourth Day of Creation, 89–92
    God's will, 49
    Gospel, 68, 92–93, 76–77, 82–83
    history of, 29–30
    hymns, 152–157
    law of rhythm, 47–48
    meditation tools, 13–15

metanoia, 47
Mid-Lent, 86–87
New Adam, 64
practice, 49, 70, 79–80, 85–86,
    87, 94–97
processions and penance, 31
purpose, 46
reliance on God, 70
renewal, 69–70
repentance, 58–59, 70
Sacramental Confession, 59
season, 46, 69
second genesis, 74
soul, 81
spring ember days, 71, 73–74
stations of the Cross, 60
structure of, 31–32
Sundays, 29, 45, 67–68, 74–76,
    80, 82, 86, 88
symbolism of mountain, 77
temptation in desert, 69
themes, 68–70, 77–79, 83–85, 93–94
third genesis, 80
traditions of, 3
training of the will, 49
Transfiguration of Christ, 77, 78
True Will, 49
The way of the Cross meditation,
    60–61
Lenten Fast, 50
    modern fast, 55–56
    to participate in life of Christ, 52–53
    to practice disciplining, 51, 52
    screen fasting, 54–55
    time of purification, 53
    traditional fast, 53–54
    withdrawal from Physical Plane,
        50–51
Leo, 119
    feast of Pentecost, 133
    Lesser Rogation, 134
    Second Creation, 133
life
    "the bread of Life", 94
    marked in seven-year cycles, 92
    phases of, 92
    spiritual life, 12, 100

liturgical prayer, 23
The Liturgical Year (Gueranger), 46, 145
liturgical year, 32, 46
The Lord's prayer, 148
The Lost Books of the Bible (Platt, Jr.), 13

magic, 5, 7
The Magic of Catholicism
    (Brother, A.D.A.), 147
Magnificat, 150
Saint Mark, 83, 135
The Mass, 7
Material Plane, 12
material world, 79
Maundy Thursday, 110. *See also* Holy
    Week; Lent; Paschal Supper
  altars, 111
  foot washing, 110, 112–113
  Last Supper, 110
  meditation, 113–115
  new commandment, 110
  Pange Lingua Gloriosi, 152–154
  Psalm for Triduum, 111–112
meditation
  Easter, 131–133
  Good Friday, 117–118
  Holy Saturday, 120–125
  Holy Week, 109
  Maundy Thursday, 113–115
  mindfulness, 22
  to prayer, 23
  Septuagesima, 36, 38
  spring ember days, 73–74
  upon Rose, 95–97
  The way of the Cross meditation,
    60–61
message-bearers, 72
metanoia, 47, 58
Michael, archangel, 125
Michaelmas, 2
Saint Michael prayer, 151
mindfulness meditation, 22
mind, plane of, 11
Misererei Mei, 157–159
Mithra, 9
mithraea, 9

Moon, 129–130
Moses, 79
mountain, 77–78
Mount Athos, 77
Mount Fuji, 77
Mount Hakusan, 77
Mount Olympus, 77
Mount Sinai, 77
Mount Tabor, 79
Mount Tateyama, 77
Muses, 6
Mysteries, 7
Mystery of Eleusis, 9
*Mystical Meditations on the Christian
    collects* (Dion Fortune), 147

Neoplatonic view, 78–79
New Adam, 64, 106. *See also* Christ (Jesus)
new commandment, 110
New Earth, 130
New Heaven, 130
new human. *See* Christ (Jesus)
Noetic Plane. *See* mind, plane of
nous, 47, 52, 63–64

Occult, 11
Oculi Sunday, 80
Odin, 21
Odyssey (Homer), 22
Olympians, 78
Origen, 62, 76
Orpheus, 9
Osiris, 9
"Ostara", goddess, 128

pagan gods, 78
Pange Lingua Gloriosi, 152–154
pasch, 93
Pascha, 128. *See also* Last Supper
Paschal Supper, 131
Paschaltide, 33, 133–134. *See also*
    Ascension
passion(s), 8, 49, 70, 97–98
The Passion of the Christ (Gibbson), 97
Passion Sunday, 97. *See also* Lent
  blessing of palms, 106–107

ceremony for blessing of branches, 107–108
Friday of Sorrows, 103
genesis, 100, 106
gospel reading, 101, 108
Holy Week, 105, 109
Palm Sunday, 105
passion, 98–100
Passiontide, 97
practice, 103–108
Seven Sorrows of Mary, 103, 104–105
spiritual life, 100
themes of, 101
Passiontide, 4
passive force, 98–99
Saint Paul, 89, 99
penal substitution theory, 3
penitential seasons, 2
Pentecost, 3, 31, 32, 139–140.
    See also Paschaltide
Persephone, goddess, 9
Phaedo and *Phaedrus*, 120
Physical Plane. *See* Material Plane
Pilate, Pontius, 59, 60, 61, 98
planes, 11–12
Planes of Being, 3
Plato, 52, 62, 76, 78, 81, 93, 94, 119, 120
Platt, Jr., R. H., 13
Polish *zur*, 30
Porphyry of Tyre, 100
prayer(s)
    Fatima prayer, 23, 27, 151
    Saint Francis, 23, 27, 40, 152
    Glory Be, 18, 27, 125, 149
    Guardian angel prayer, 151
    Hail, Holy Queen, 150–151
    Hail Mary, 18, 148–149
    Holy Spirit prayer, 149
    The Lord's prayer, 148
    Magnificat, 150
    Saint Michael prayer, 151
pre-Lent. *See* Gesimatide
pretzel, 30
Psychic Plane. *See* soul—plane of
psychoactive brews in
    medieval West, 51

Quasimodo, 133–134
Quinquegesima, 33
egregore, 39
Forgiveness Sunday, 38–39
great forgiveness ritual, 39–40
Practice for, 39

rational soul, 81
Redemption, 32
re-enchantment, 2
    of time, 3
Regulus, 119
reliance on God, 70
Reminiscere Sunday, 74
renewal, 69–70
repent, 58
repentance, 58–59, 70
The Republic (Plato), 52
Resurrection, 63, 129
    of Christ, 1, 3, 79
    and Salvation, 3
The Rituale Romanum, 146
Rose Sunday, 88–89
Rosicrucian Cosmo-Conception
    (Heindel), 146
"rule", 89–90

sabbath, Jewish, 129
sackcloth, 62
Sacramental
    churches, 1, 10
    Confession, 42, 59
The Sacramental Magic of Advent
    (Thomas), 3, 4, 17
Sacraments, 7
    of Confession and Communion, 10
    The Rituale, 146
    seven Sacraments, 10
    works of magic, 7
sacred items, 14
saint(s), 5–6
    Augustine, 72
    Francis prayer, 23, 27, 40, 152
    Mark, 83, 135
    Michael prayer, 151
    Paul, 89, 99

Simon of Cyrene, 60
Veronica, 60
The Saint Andrew Daily Missal, with Vespers for Sundays and Feasts (Lefebvre), 145
Santa Claus, 129
Satan, 82, 84, 119, 125
   and Hades, 121–124
Scrutiny Sunday, 80
Second Coming, 32
Second Person of Holy Trinity, 130
Septuagesima, 3, 30, 33, 34
   meditation, 36, 38
   practice for Septuagesima week, 35–36
   traditional gospel reading, 35
   understanding parables, 35–36
The Seven Habits of Highly Effective People (Covey), 56
seven Sacraments, 10
Seven Sorrows of Mary, 103, 104–105
Sexagesima, 33, 36–38
Shrove Tuesday, 41–44
Sign of the Cross, 19, 21
Saint Simon of Cyrene, 60
sin, 12
Socrates, 78
Sorrowful Mysteries, 69
soul, 52, 81
   Adam and Eve, 63
   Aristotelian view, 81
   disordered, 52
   "eye of the soul", 62
   imprisoned within bodies, 119
   individual, 75
   plane of, 11
   rational, 81
   symbolism of water as, 75
   Universal Soul, 75
   vegetable form, 81–82, 91
   vital, 81
   well-ordered soul, 52
Sphere of Protection, 21
spirit(s)
   earth-bound, 79
   evil, 84

The Holy Spirit prayer, 149
   other than God, 5
spiritual
   alchemy, 33
   life, 12, 71, 100
   and temporal power, 94–95
Spy Wednesday, 110
Stabat Mater, 154–157
Sunday, 29, 31, 129. *See also* Passion Sunday
   Brand Sunday, 67, 69
   as creation and redemption, 32
   Dead Sunday, 86
   Easter Sunday, 81
   Forgiveness Sunday, 38–39
   Invocabit Sunday, 67
   Laetare Sunday, 86, 88, 95
   Oculi Sunday, 80
   Reminiscere Sunday, 74
   Rose Sunday, 88–89
   Scrutiny Sunday, 80
   as Seventh Day of creation, 81
   six Sundays of Lent, 29, 45, 67–68, 74–76, 88
   Third Sunday of Advent, 88
   Transfiguration Sunday, 74
   Whit Sunday, 140
The Sun, 129. *See* Christ (Jesus)
symbolism
   of Christ, 34, 125, 129
   of mountain, 77
   seasonal, 13
   of water, 75, 76

temptation, 70–71. *See also* Lent
temptation of Christ in the desert, 68–69
Tenebrae services, 110
third eye, 62
Third Sunday of Advent, 88
Three Books of Occult Philosophy (Agrippa), 146
thymos, 52, 81
Timaeus (Plato), 93
time, 2, 91–92
The tomb, 125
Transfiguration of Christ, 77

Transfiguration Sunday, 74
True Adam, 81
true Heaven, 120
true Human Being, 81
True Will, 8, 49

unity, plane of, 11
Universal Soul, 75

Vegetable Soul, 81–82
Saint Veronica, 60
Via Dolorosa, 59–60
visualization, 19–20
vital soul, 81

Waite, A. E., 21
water, 75, 76, 80, 86

Waters above the Heavens, 75
The way of the Cross meditation,
    60–61
Weber, M., 2
Weiser, F. X., 146
well-ordered soul, 52
Whit Monday, 140
Whit Sunday, 140
Will of God, 8, 62–63, 64, 85
working space, 13

Yang and Yin, 98

zazen, 22
Zeus, 21, 78
Zodiac signs, 90
zur, 30

www.ingramcontent.com/pod-product-compliance
Lightning Source LLC
Chambersburg PA
CBHW050929240426
43671CB00020B/2970